More Praise for *Authentic Conv*

"After thirty-five years working in ne
'school readiness' advocate, I wished
It would have helped so much. Its basic theme of honest, respectful
conversations is the answer to so much in business and in life."

> —David Lawrence Jr., President, The Early Childhood
> Initiative Foundation, and retired publisher, *The Miami
> Herald*

"The Showkeirs have written a book that gives us the tools for conversations that can help us create a shared purpose and the future we hope for. This authentic approach is essential not only for business results but for any conversation that is important to you."

> —Nancy Light, Senior Associate Director of Philanthropy,
> The Nature Conservancy, Maine Chapter

"This book is for everyone, from the CEO to the everyday employee, who is serious about working in an organization in which every person has a deep personal commitment to the success of the business. The concepts and practical steps outlined in this book are easy to understand and are a genuine source of sustainable competitive advantage. This book offers us hope."

> —Jim Burke, Regional Director of Human Resources,
> Asia Pacific, Watson Wyatt Worldwide

"If you believe that conversations change the world and if you have a passion for organizations that work, you will want this book. This book has the combination of relevance, inspiration, and actionable steps that I seek in books."

> —John Schuster, Principal, Schuster Kane Alliance,
> and author of *The Power of Open-Book Management* and
> *Answering Your Call*

"This book is about sharing the truth with each other in ways that build effective relationships and improve business results. It is not a fairy tale but an honest, hard-hitting book. And it's not just for leaders or managers—it is for everyone in your organization. If you want to compete successfully in the world marketplace, you need *Authentic Conversations*."

> —Dr. Kent M. Keith, CEO, Greenleaf Center for Servant-
> Leadership, and author of *Anyway: The Paradoxical
> Commandments*

"I can't remember the last time I was this excited about a book on corporate cultures and leadership. *Authentic Conversations* gets to the heart of what is really going on in organizations, presents persuasive business reasons for change, and puts forth a proven strategy to get on with unleashing the organization's buried and dormant core potential. It left me wanting more."

—Patrick J. Banks, PhD, President, Banks International, LLC

"The Showkeirs' take on using conversations for cultural transformation is refreshing and eminently logical. They challenge much of the conventional wisdom about managing people. This book teaches us how to intrinsically inspire individuals to choose to succeed."

—Bob Gremillion, Executive Vice President, Tribune Publishing Company

"The Showkeirs' new book envisions organizations where employees treat each other as business partners, colleagues, and trusted advisors, allowing the wisdom of the organization to emerge. For leaders ready to share power in order to build an organization that is stronger, more responsive, more flexible, and more focused on serving customers, this book is a field manual for changing cultures. It is a must read."

—Melvin D. Dowdy, PhD, Executive Director, Center for Organizational Excellence, Bon Secours Richmond Health System

"*Authentic Conversations* is one of the most important books I've read in years. It makes a compelling case for the great benefits—both for people and for organizations—that can come from engaging in true conversation."

—Larry C. Spears, President and CEO, The Spears Center for Servant-Leadership, Inc.

"*Authentic Conversations* gives us a chance to renew and revive a lost art and essential foundational element so our society can be viable. Additionally, this book gives us models for how to have conversations for those who have never been exposed to an authentic conversation."

—Corwin Harper, Senior Vice President/Area Manager, Kaiser Permanente

Authentic Conversations

Authentic Conversations

Moving from Manipulation to Truth and Commitment

Jamie Showkeir and Maren Showkeir

Foreword by Margaret J. Wheatley

BK

Berrett–Koehler Publishers, Inc.
San Francisco
a BK Business book

Berrett-Koehler Publishers, Inc.
235 Montgomery Street, Suite 650
San Francisco, CA 94104-2916
Tel: (415) 288-0260   Fax: (415) 362-2512   www.bkconnection.com

Ordering Information
Quantity sales. Special discounts are available on quantity purchases by corporations, associations, and others. For details, contact the "Special Sales Department" at the Berrett-Koehler address above.
Individual sales. Berrett-Koehler publications are available through most bookstores. They can also be ordered directly from Berrett-Koehler: Tel: (800) 929-2929; Fax: (802) 864-7626; www.bkconnection.com
Orders for college textbook/course adoption use. Please contact Berrett-Koehler: Tel: (800) 929-2929; Fax: (802) 864-7626.
Orders by U.S. trade bookstores and wholesalers. Please contact Ingram Publisher Services, Tel: (800) 509-4887; Fax: (800) 838-1149; E-mail: customer.service@ingrampublisherservices.com; or visit www.ingrampublisherservices.com/Ordering for details about electronic ordering.

Berrett-Koehler and the BK logo are registered trademarks of Berrett-Koehler Publishers, Inc.

Printed in the United States of America
Berrett-Koehler books are printed on long-lasting acid-free paper. When it is available, we choose paper that has been manufactured by environmentally responsible processes. These may include using trees grown in sustainable forests, incorporating recycled paper, minimizing chlorine in bleaching, or recycling the energy produced at the paper mill.

Library of Congress Cataloging-in-Publication Data
Showkeir, Jamie, 1952–
    Authentic conversations : moving from manipulation to truth and commitment / Jamie Showkeir, Maren Showkeir.
        p. cm.
    Includes bibliographical references and index.
    ISBN 978-1-57675-595-2 (pbk. : alk. paper)
    1. Communication in organizations. 2. Interpersonal relations.
3. Organizational behavior. I. Showkeir, Maren, 1957– II. Title.
    HD30.3.S553 2008
    658.4'5—dc22
    2008018072

First Edition
13 12 11 10 09 08   10 9 8 7 6 5 4 3 2 1

Interior Design: Valerie Brewster
Cover Design: The Book Designers/Ian
Production Service: Linda Jupiter Productions

Copy Editor: Lunaea Weatherstone
Proofreader: Henrietta Bensussen
Indexer: Medea Minnich

Contents

Dedication

Joel P. Henning

June 12, 1939–May 30, 2001

Joel was not a saint and writing about him as if he were would do no justice to his memory. Those who knew him best described him as difficult. They would say that to have a relationship with him meant doing it on his terms. He viewed voice mail, for instance, as "an invitation to return the call, not an obligation." He often described himself seriously, despite his impish grin, as a "down person, who actually likes winter in New Jersey."

Even so, his thinking and work were full of hope and light—and pragmatism. Joel found usefulness in lofty ideas only to the extent they could enhance organizations and life in practical ways. He was well acquainted with frustration and disillusionment, and yet he believed to the core of his soul that choosing optimism and commitment in the face of disappointment was the only true way to live.

In the roles he served throughout his life—priest, assistant school superintendent, consultant, writer, father, friend, and partner—Joel cared deeply about making a difference. "I would rather be useful than helpful," he once said to me. I asked him why. He replied, "Sometimes being useful means having to say things that are not always helpful."

Joel was my mentor, friend, colleague, and teacher. He captured my heart, my imagination, and my pragmatic interest in life and in organizations. I may be the only person alive who read his entire dissertation—three times—and actually enjoyed it. He used to call me "Brother Love," a nickname born of his favorite song, Neil Diamond's "Brother Love's Traveling Salvation Show." On hundreds of mornings, as we took our last gulps of coffee, he would say to me, "Brother Love, it's time to get on with it." In those moments, I felt an overwhelming sense of the importance of our work. We saw ourselves as bringing love into environments that traditionally scoffed at matters of the heart.

Working with Joel, I learned how to "get hold of the frame in the room" and "stop facilitating the craziness." He taught me how to get people engaged and constantly admonished me, "Stop talking so much, for God's sake!" With his guidance, I began learning to turn my strident self down.

Most of all, Joel strove to make me understand that *who I am is enough*. Just about the time I felt like I was starting to get it, Joel suddenly died.

One winter evening in 1997, just as I was sitting down for dinner, Joel called me from his vacation in Mexico. "I have been thinking more about the connection between conversations and organizational culture," he said. "Do you want to talk?" We did, for nearly ninety minutes. After we hung up, I sat down and wrote eight pages based on our conversation. That was the genesis of this book.

I think what is written here represents the best of his thinking. It is a reflection and explication of what Joel and I learned working together over many years. It also contains the best of what Maren and I have learned together. We believe this book would meet Joel's test for being "useful." In that vein, we dedicate it to Joel and his continuing presence in the work and the lives of all who knew him.

"Brother Love, it's time to get on with it."

Jamie Showkeir

An Invitation

by Margaret J. Wheatley

In 2002, I published *Turning to One Another: Simple Conversations to Restore Hope to the Future*, and went public with this statement: "I believe we can change the world if we just start talking to one another again." In the years since I made this rather simplistic albeit well-founded claim, the world has only grown more dark and complex. Because of this, I now believe in the power of conversation even more. It is a crucial and simple means to reverse the dangerous societal slide of increasing fragmentation and fear of "the other." This slide will continue until we sit down and begin to talk with each other. If we can do this, if we can approach those we know and those we don't know with curiosity and anticipation, we will discover that they are just human beings with similar hopes, fears, motivations, and dreams.

These days, very few people remember the pleasure of being in good conversations, especially in the workplace. We race past one another at tornado speed, frantic to get through our ever-growing list of tasks, consumed by and consuming meaninglessness. Nearly three-fourths of American workers are disengaged, which means they're doing the minimum of what's required and not offering anything extra—no creativity, caring, or responsibility. I place the blame for this terrible apathy and indifference squarely at the feet of command-and-control leadership. When people are bossed around, treated like robots, and discarded casually, any sensible person disengages. Why waste our human potential on a place or person that has no regard for us?

And there's no sign that it's going to get any better in organizations. Fear has become the primary motivator. Turning people against one another in aggressively competitive ways is now common practice. Speed is the synonym for productivity. Time to think has simply disappeared. We don't learn from our experiences, we just do the same thing over and over again, only faster. When things go wrong or people refuse to engage, leaders get more demanding, more controlling, more imperious, and more destructive.

The destructive character of so many workplaces shows up in our bodies as well as our spirits. Stress-related illnesses account for at least one-third of worker absenteeism. Sleeping disorders, anxiety disorders, bad stomachs, bad backs—these are all signs of a society under acute stress. In 2007, fewer people took vacations from work than ever before; in one study, 40 percent of workers didn't take vacation. In another, one-third of those who took vacation stayed connected to their offices electronically.

How much longer will this descent into ill health and ill-functioning organizations continue?

Into this current insanity comes this very sane book. This is a thoughtful and patient book, filled with examples drawn from years of experience. Its clear and simple processes truly show how we could stop this deterioration in the workplace and become fully human at work again. The authors remind us of basic truths about how human beings work well together—that we're adults, that we work best with intrinsic motivators of contribution and meaning, that we're creative, that we have a need for community, that work needs to be engaging, that people behave responsibly when they care, that conversation is the way we think well together.

The gift of this book is that it gives us a pathway to the future. If we begin to engage one another in earnest and honest conversation, if we slow down sufficiently to reengage with the purpose of our work, we can find our way out of the messes we've created by ignoring each other and retreating into fearful isolation.

However, let us remember current realities. The wisdom expressed here has receded so far into the background of how we work together that this book is nothing less than a revolutionary manifesto. Like all real revolutions, this one reclaims what is noble and good about humans. It offers us hope for a different, more positive future, and it embodies an idealism that can inspire us to do all we can to bring about this change.

If you don't already know that it's time for revolution, this book will awaken you to this fact with its clarity and experience. We simply cannot let this disintegration go any farther. We cannot continue to work without being engaged. We cannot continue to pursue our separating, frantic ways and expect our lives and future to have any goodness in them.

The major tactic of this revolution is simple, straightforward, and absolutely nonviolent: Get people talking to each other. Engage in meaningful conversations. Practice nondenial—look truthfully at what's going on. Expect people to respond creatively. Expect generosity. Expect things to improve.

Why would we refuse such an opportunity? Why wouldn't we all rush to embrace this simple but profound tactic for creating real change through hosting conversations that matter? Why wouldn't we absorb this book and start right now?

I don't know your personal answers to these questions, but what I've observed is that, generally, people are terrified to begin a conversation. Many, many people comment that it takes extraordinary courage to begin a conversation. And they're right. What was a simple and natural human experience—talking together—has become a scary prospect. As our fear of the other has grown, as polarization has driven us farther apart, as dominating power over others has increased, conversation seems impossible.

Further proof that we're talking about a revolution.

So it's up to us. If we want the future to be different from the present, we have to be the ones to begin the conversation. I can promise good things: We will be surprised and delighted by the capacities that emerge when we take the time to speak honestly and thoughtfully to one another. We will be astonished by what we can create when we're engaged in authentic conversations.

I hope you will accept this invitation to the revolution.

Preface

Typical workplace conversations are so common they almost seem invisible. They are so ingrained in our daily life that we often don't realize how deeply they influence our experience of the world. Conversations are more significant than we are aware of, more powerful than we acknowledge. They are much like breathing.

When is the last time you spared a thought for breathing? Why would you? You inhale and take in oxygen. Your exhalation releases carbon dioxide. This instinctive action keeps you alive, and while you know this, you rarely ponder it. You have been doing it since you were born and so has everyone you know, so what is there to learn about breathing?

Yoga practitioners, however, would say there is plenty to ponder. They have a completely different perspective and relationship with breathing. Through study and experience, they come to an awareness and understanding of the breath, and then harness its power. Before we began studying yoga, for instance, we didn't realize that breathing could create energy or calm the mind. Through years of practice, we have learned techniques that can generate internal heat or cool the body. We have a fresh perspective of the importance of receiving (inhale) and letting go (exhale). By focusing deeply on our breathing, we are able to create a stillness that facilitates meditation. As we have become more aware of what breath can do, we have developed an enormous appreciation and respect for its significance and its power.

So it is with the power of conversations. In this book, we hope to create for you an awareness of how daily conversations create, reveal, sustain, or change organizational culture. We explore the significant role culture has in facilitating healthy relationships and creating business results. Our premise is that true and lasting changes to organizational culture cannot occur unless people understand how traditional conversations stymie growth and erode commitment.

If you continue reading, and of course we hope you will, it is likely you will recognize people you know—your coworkers, your supervisors, senior leaders, and others. But please make no mistake, we wrote this book for *you*. If you take it seriously, it's likely to make you feel a little uncomfortable. What we write about here entails risk and may seem overwhelming. Engaging in authentic conversation is extremely challenging, and even those who commit to it can find it difficult to do consistently. We have joked that we should have titled this book *The Dangerous Book for Adults*.

We have all grown up in a culture where conversation is often viewed as a tool for getting what we want, for winning others over to our points of view. You know this from personal experience and so do we. For twenty years, we have worked with clients who desired to gain the benefits that can be derived from using authentic conversations. We feel passionately that abandoning manipulation and engaging others authentically is the right thing to do. It is a major part of our life's work. And still we struggle, every single day, to get it right.

Even so, we believe that by evaluating and adopting the commitments and applying the skills written about here, you can create new conversations with others right now. The type of organization in which you work doesn't matter nor does the position you hold. With new conversations, any organization can transform itself into a place where the demand for business results can be harmonized with the individual's need to find meaning and purpose at work.

People have myriad choices as they browse for books about conversation and communication in libraries, bookstores, and on the Internet. We understand that we are entering a crowded market. We think our book has a major differentiating feature: we focus specifically on changing conversations as the *primary* means for changing an organization's culture from parent–child to adult–adult. We offer concrete steps for doing so and ground them in a solid, market-oriented business argument. We also focus on the soulful questions of intention, purpose, and meaning.

Among other things, we advocate *choosing accountability for the whole* as the overriding frame for managing conversations. Many books take the approach of improving or changing conversations as a matter of self-interest or self-development. We emphasize the necessity of treating others' points of view and life experiences as the fundamental reality. We don't advocate authentic conversations as a means for self-promotion, getting ahead, or getting what you want, but as a way of engaging *everyone.* This is about interdependence and collaboration, caring about the other's success as much as you do your own, and increasing the likelihood that we will all benefit.

Other authors we know espouse kinder, subtler, or more benevolent manipulative techniques to "sell" others on a point of view or to get "buy-in" for new programs, processes, or policies. Many of these books are aimed at advising leaders to position information and/or align what they say with another's self-interest. They advocate "motivational" techniques for winning employees' support for goals formulated at the top of the organization. These concepts are grounded in reliance on the traditional hierarchy, conversations used for manipulation and effect, and the associated lines of communication that mostly flow downward. We reject both the concepts and their associated tactics.

The premise we offer is that a chasm exists between compliance and commitment, in their very nature and in the results they yield. For commitment to be authentic, people must choose. Unless "no" is a legitimate option, the answer "yes" has no meaning. Leaders in organizations often say they want commitment but center their conversations on merely gaining compliance. Because the front line in any organization is where the core work gets done, commitment there, not compliance, is essential for good results. Real improvement efforts in any organization must be engaged *first* at the front line. Those in the front line must be treated as the complex and capable human beings they are, acknowledging their perspectives as legitimate and engaging them in a way that takes this into account. Doing so generates widespread commitment, meaning, purpose, and improved business results. We make this case using real examples to support our premise, and we offer concrete, practical ways to create and sustain this transformation.

Most of today's enterprises have their organizational roots in the thinking of the industrial age, which views people in a mechanistic way and treats them as parts in a larger machine. Parent–child conversations and cultures have existed throughout the ages, and traditional management structures and reporting relationships reinforce them. This can be seen in the ways people typically talk to each other every day at work. In this book, we propose a radical new way of looking at how people in the workplace get work done, and we give sound business reasons for doing so. Along with like-minded authors such as Chris Argyris, Peter Block, Alfie Kohn, John Schuster, Meg Wheatley, Danah Zohar, Ian Marshall, and many others, we advocate abolishing command-and-control systems in favor of systems that rely on widespread literacy, contribution, collaboration, and commitment. Creating new, authentic conversations is essential to move organizations in this new direction.

We explore the issues rooted in questions such as:

- How does the organization move from a parent–child culture to an adult–adult culture?

- How can you recognize the damage caused by manipulative conversations?

- How can you learn to engage in authentic conversations based on collaboration and partnership?

- How do you eliminate traditional leadership conversations aimed at caretaking and control?

- How can you engage people in ways that value their knowledge, experience, and contribution?

- How can you create an organizational culture that maximizes the potential of the entire organization?

These questions and others addressed in this book are relevant to all organizations accountable for results today and in the foreseeable future.

Although this look at conversations has myriad applications, it was written with a workplace audience in mind. Among the people who will find this book useful are core workers, supervisors, managers, team leaders, and those in executive roles. It will also be useful to individuals and professionals in human resources, organization development, and other staff groups responsible for internal development or for leading development activities in the larger organization. Those who are doing life, career, and executive coaching and mentoring will find it relevant, along with those who study organizations or teach others about how they are structured.

Trainers and coaches can use this book in two specific ways: First, they can begin to incorporate the concepts, commitments, and skills into existing programs for supervisors, managers, and executives, as well as whole teams and departments. Interpersonal skills training, communications skills training, and other types of training can be adapted to include this content. Second, trainers and facilitators can use these skills when dealing with groups as a way of engaging authentic conversations in the room, regardless of the content of the meeting, seminar, or workshop. Incorporating the commitments and skills in this book will make even highly skilled and experienced trainers and facilitators more effective.

In the first half of the book, we analyze traditional conversations using real examples gleaned from more than twenty years of experience. We explore the problems caused by the conventional ways people view each other at work and the common ways they talk to each other. Parent–child cultures are born when an organization values control, consistency, and predictability as the strategy for managing people. We explore how conversations are created purposely to sustain that culture and why their perpetuation profoundly inhibits organizations trying to compete in a demanding, fast-paced global arena that values flexibility, innovation, and diversity.

The second half of the book is designed to address these difficulties by offering new perspectives and specific, concrete ways to change the culture through authentic conversations. At the end of the book, we provide a guide with sample scripts for raising difficult issues, proposing a change, dealing with individual performance, introducing a mandate, seeking exceptions, creating beginnings, and more. This provides a further springboard for beginning more engaging and authentic conversations—without waiting for someone else to go first.

We emphasize the personal commitment necessary for undergoing this transformation, both as an individual and as a member of an organization. Committing to this transformation is not a one-time endeavor. A new consciousness and self-awareness are necessary for engaging others more authentically. This requires constant and consistent attention. We explore this in these pages with the hope of stimulating further exploration.

We also expose destructive behaviors such as caretaking, cynicism, and helplessness. Light is shed on the dangerous subtlety of manipulation, the importance of language, and intentions as the driver of our actions. People catch on very quickly when language and behavior don't match up with our intentions. We take on the myth that accountability can be mandated or legislated. No matter how many policies and procedures are instituted in an effort to "hold other people accountable," in the end, accountability is always a choice we make.

Finally, we outline new conversations that directly confront these things as the choices they are. Getting clear on our intentions, then aligning our speech and actions to those intentions, is the only way we can travel on the road to authentic conversations.

This book is heavily indebted to the knowledge and experience that have come out of the work of Jamie Showkeir and the late Joel Henning who in 1997, when they were managing partners at Designed Learning, created a conversations workshop for organizations looking for cultural transformation. Their premise reframes leadership as a conscious act of managing conversations for engagement, disclosure, and authenticity to promote culture change, improve business results, and create environments that harmonize work and meaning. It was born from the idea that each of us longs to contribute to something greater than ourselves, to create something real in which we can believe.

During our years of working with thousands of people, we have tried to illuminate the power of conversations and help others harness the power of being authentic. With this book, we continue that journey.

Please take a deep breath and continue reading. We are at the beginning of a new conversation.

" The Dangerous
Book for Adults "

We were consulting with a large East Coast newspaper grappling with a multimillion-dollar shortfall and the
plagues of the industry in general: declining circulation, shrinking advertising revenue, and increasing newsprint prices. The
problems of this newspaper were compounded by changes in the
region's demographics, which raised questions about whether the
paper's content was relevant to the readers in their market. Layoffs seemed inevitable. Hundreds were likely to lose their jobs.

In preparation for a large group meeting about the crisis, we
followed the publisher for an entire day as he met with small
groups of employees from advertising, circulation, production,
and the newsroom. Everyone asked similar questions: "What are
you going to do about this crisis, Joe? How are you going to fix
it?" They complained about being unable to be productive because they were so stressed about the possibility of losing their
jobs. They angrily told Joe they blamed him and other senior

managers for "getting us into this mess" and demanded to know what he was going to do about it.

Joe encouraged the employees to focus on the long term. "We will get reestablished," he assured them. "We will develop new strategies to build circulation and advertising. We will find ways to make our stories more relevant to readers. We are negotiating with corporate for leniency regarding the profit demands." All day long, we heard him give one reassuring message after another: "Don't worry, I'm going to make you safe. Don't worry, senior leaders will take care of it."

Joe was a bright, capable, and caring man. He was passionate about his job and committed to his employees. He wanted to do the right things. But in our estimation, he was saying all the wrong things. His conversations were making the situation worse. By making promises he couldn't possibly keep and sending a message to employees that they were off the hook for resolving a difficult situation, he was exacerbating the problems the company faced.

We gave him our frank assessment of the damage he had been doing. Joe, obviously taken aback, was thoughtful and silent as he contemplated our feedback.

We'll get back to Joe's story, but first let's look at why we paid such close attention to the conversations he was having with the newspaper's employees.

Conversations Create Culture

James A. Autry, businessman, author, and poet, says, "We do make things true by what we say. . . . Things and people are what we call them, because in the simplest terms, we are what we say, and others are what we say about them."

Simply put, a conversation is an exchange between two or more individuals, but that simple definition obscures a conversation's complexity. Words and language are powerful tools, and conversations are so commonplace in our daily lives that we don't pause to contemplate their inherent power.

First, conversations *reveal* what we see in the world and what *meaning* we attach to what we see. Second, as Autry says, we *name* things and *create reality*. Third, we *invite* others to see what we see, the way we see it. And fourth, through conversations we either *sustain or change* the meaning of what we see. All these things play a commanding role in creating and defining an organization's culture.

The term "culture" refers to the universal capacity that human beings have to classify, codify, and communicate their experiences symbolically. In other words, culture dictates our beliefs, behavior, language, and social interaction. Nonverbal communication and unwritten rules play a large role here.

Edgar Schein, a professor at the MIT Sloan School for management and the man credited with coining the term "corporate culture," talks about culture as being a pattern of shared basic assumptions. Schein defined organizational culture as "the specific collection of values and norms that are shared by people and groups in an organization and that control the way they interact with each other and with stakeholders outside the organization." He wrote that these norms "prescribe appropriate behavior by employees and control the behavior of organizational members towards one another."

Culture tells us what is acceptable and unacceptable. It alerts us to whether it is okay to show up a little late for a meeting, how we should be dressed when we arrive, and whether bringing up difficult issues in the room will be viewed favorably. It influences how we treat each other, talk to each other, and is a factor in the way we view and interact with our coworkers and customers.

Culture shows up as a similarity in the way people behave at work, regardless of their rank, title, or serial number. As Margaret

J. Wheatley writes in *Leadership and the New Science*, "I am often struck by eerily similar behaviors exhibited by people in an organization, whether I'm meeting with a factory floor employee or a senior executive. I might detect a recurring penchant for secrecy or for openness, for name-calling or for thoughtfulness. These recurring patterns of behavior are what many call the culture of an organization."

Changing the Culture Requires New Conversations

The overarching creators and carriers of an organization's culture are the conversations in which the members of that organization engage. The ways people see and talk about things such as cynicism, hope, helplessness, and resourcefulness, their customers, and the work itself reflect organizational culture. Statements about the culture are seen in what we say as well as through our behavior. Culture influences decisions such as whether to share or withhold information, whether it's more important to defer to a person's position instead of authentically stating a point of view, and whether we see our coworkers as collaborators or competitors.

In an organization where power is concentrated at the top, compliance is highly valued, and parent–child roles are established, the cultural norm looks like this: "When my boss tells me to do something, even if it doesn't make sense to me, I don't push back. Dissent marks me as uncooperative and threatens my future." Or "When my morale is low, it is management's job to figure out what's wrong, find the solution, and implement changes. People's unhappiness is a statement of faulty leadership."

In an organization where business literacy, choice, and accountability are distributed widely and deeply, where flexibility and innovation are highly valued and the dominant roles are adult–adult, the culture norm is "When I see something is wrong,

I want to attend to it. I am expected to attend to it and I am accountable for doing so. My boss and coworkers expect me to push back and challenge their thinking. Dissent and accountability are the lubricants of this organization."

Conversation is the primary way of learning and sharing cultural norms, especially those ways that are informal and implicit. Messages are transmitted both in the words we use and in the relationship dynamics that drive how we talk to each other.

For this reason, common workplace conversations can sabotage any attempt at significant organizational change. How we talk to each other in business settings and the way we deliberate decisions are revealing. In addition, some of the most powerful conversations take place outside the boardrooms, the auditoriums, and the meeting rooms. They happen in restrooms, coffee rooms, during smoke breaks, in people's offices, on the assembly line, and during chance encounters in the hall. They continue in bars and cafés after work. Those ordinary conversations that people have thousands of times a day ultimately define the culture.

Establishing *new* conversations is the most effective way—and the most underutilized—to create ongoing, long-lasting change in our lives, our organizations, and society. New conversations require us to see each other in a different way, and create an awareness of our role in perpetuating habits and behaviors that don't serve us well.

To illustrate, let's return to our story about Joe and the conversations he had been having with employees. This is the feedback we gave him before his big meeting with employees: "In all the meetings you had with people today, you were reassuring them that things would turn around and that you were going to make it okay. Joe, how are you going to do that?" In the type of culture we advocate, it is likely that one or more people would have already asked this question directly in the small group meetings.

But the existing culture did not support asking this difficult question of senior management. Nor did the culture encourage introspection about individual accountability.

Joe was silent for a while, and then he finally said, "Well, I *want* to make it okay. Everyone is *expecting* me to make it okay. If I tell people the truth, that I don't know what the solution is yet, this paper might fall apart today, right now. It is my responsibility to figure things out and to reassure people."

We asked, "Who are these people you're talking about? Are they children or are they adults?" From our perspective, he was stuck in a traditional way of looking at things and choosing the same old conversations to talk about a difficult situation. He was reinforcing the parent–child relationship embedded in the culture. By choosing words of reassurance, by promising to define and solve the problems and telling employees they shouldn't worry about the company's future, he was treating employees as children who needed caretaking and protecting. However, what he needed in these circumstances were capable adults who would participate in creating a successful organization and own their accountability for finding solutions. We suggested he try a new conversation by changing his view of the people who show up to work every day and the words he chose when he talked to them.

First, we advised him to stop sugarcoating the situation and tell employees the truth about the difficult circumstances the newspaper faced.

Second, we asked him to stop promising them a safe and secure future that he knew was impossible to deliver.

And finally, we advised that he help employees realize that their issues of safety and security were something they were going to have to manage for themselves. In fact, they were the only ones who could.

Joe found our suggestions daunting. He wrestled with the ramifications. But at the end of the day, he stood up in front of a large group of disappointed, scared, and angry employees who were looking for reassurance, and he had a new conversation with them.

He began, "I have been doing a lot of thinking since our departmental meetings today, and I have some tough things to say to you that I didn't say when we met earlier." He then explained clearly and directly the full gravity of the situation they all faced in making the newspaper profitable in the current market. He admitted that he had made the situation worse by implying he had answers to those difficult issues when he didn't and by reassuring employees that things would be all right when he couldn't be sure. He was clear with them about the costs of failure and said he needed them to begin taking responsibility for finding the answers. Joe was emphatic about the necessity of everyone working together to turn the situation around.

He finished by saying this: "The final thing I have to say is the most difficult. I can do nothing about your happiness. I can do nothing to make you feel safe, and I can do nothing to make you feel secure. Those things are in *your* hands. You will have to choose what you are going to do to account for your own future here and the future of this newspaper. I will do everything I can, and I hope you will too, but stop tap-dancing on my head about your happiness as if I were accountable for it. I am not."

There was a moment of tense and bewildered silence. Then the employees spontaneously stood up and applauded—for a long time. It was a crazy moment of relief. They had been told the truth for the first time in years. Joe had acknowledged that they were adults, and he had talked to them as adults. He made it clear that he could not resolve the paper's problems by himself. In effect, he was saying, "I am going to stop the empty, reassuring message. Nobody believes it anyway. Let's start getting straight about what is going on here."

It was a wonderful moment for the organization. Joe stopped the old conversation and created a new, authentic way of talking to the employees. He changed the culture in the room.

Organizational Culture and the Business

When we begin working with a client organization, we assess the culture and other things by interviewing people throughout the company. One of the first questions we ask is "What is it like to work here?"

When enough people say, "This is a difficult place to work. The pace is hectic and demanding, they don't really care what I think. Nothing ever changes and I feel like all they want me to do is show up and do what they say," we can draw some solid conclusions about the culture. We can deduce that the work is fast-paced and people work long hours, but they don't understand why and they don't like it. We hear that they are afraid to speak out or feel unheard if they do. They feel their ability to contribute is limited and attempts to overcome dissatisfaction have failed. They feel like victims and justify those feelings. We can conclude that the culture is riddled with parent–child conversations.

The ways in which people view change are also signals of organizational culture. People say things like this: "When someone suggests a change, someone else says, 'We tried that before, and it didn't work.' Pretty soon everyone is talking about what happened in the past and how change never works rather than the proposal on the table."

Statements such as these tell us a lot. They tell us that people in the organization have been disappointed by change efforts, and the culture is marked by a lack of hope and optimism. People see themselves as victims of an inept organization, and the culture accepts and supports their helplessness. And because their conversations are centered on disappointment, injustice, and not being taken seriously, rather than the demands of the business, we can conclude that serious issues that affect success aren't being addressed in the way they should be.

In one large health care company where we consulted, for example, employees who worked in billing were being hammered by a series of difficult business problems that threatened to shut the department down. Outsourcing was a possibility. During our interviews with employees, most of their comments centered on issues such as how unfriendly some of the supervisors were, whose turn it was to clean the coffee station, and whether the window blinds should be open or closed. They said very little that led us to believe they were concerned about, much less actively trying to solve, serious business problems that threatened their employment.

The first, most critical step to creating a healthier, more productive culture is to change the conversations. Changing a conversation in the moment can change the culture in the room, the way Joe did when he told the truth about a difficult situation. Changing the culture in the room in any given moment is the best any of us can do. If new conversations change the culture in the room enough times and in enough rooms—the organization's culture *will* change.

We can learn to talk about cynicism, for example, as the choice that it is rather than as a predetermined outcome of disappointment. By having that conversation, we can reveal what we see and what we make of the choice for cynicism. We can invite others to see it in the same way, and by doing so, we seize an opportunity to confront cynicism and change the point of view in the room.

Changing the culture with new conversations can create a more mature, resilient organization with a capacity for creativity, innovation, and transformation in the face of unyielding market-place demands. Through new conversations, we can establish organizations that people believe in, where they take accountability for the success of the whole, where people find meaning in the work they do and achieve the necessary results to succeed.

A New Conversation

Joe's new conversation with the newspaper employees had four powerful elements that are not typically heard at traditional organizations:

> *First, he honestly acknowledged the problems and named the difficult issues.* The newspaper was in deep trouble; he didn't have all the answers and did not expect the answers to come fast or easily.

> *Second, he owned his contribution to the difficulty.* He admitted he had clouded issues by understating the crisis and offering empty reassurances to those who should have been engaged in finding solutions. He acknowledged he had wanted to make people feel safe and secure, even when he knew he couldn't.

> *Third, he stated the risks and acknowledged the possibility of things not working out.* He was telling it to them straight when he said, "I don't know how we are going to solve these problems."

> *Fourth, he presented them with a choice.* He confronted the fact that everyone had a choice to make about what they were going to do and how they were going to face the future.

Business Implications of Telling the Truth

For Joe, the business implications of telling the truth were enormous. Everyone in the room that day was looking for leadership from the boss—and he had a choice to make. On the one hand, he could continue caretaking and encourage employees to look to him and senior management for answers and reassurance. But if he did that, people in the organization would remain stuck, unable to act for themselves. They would get the message that they were off the hook for finding solutions. In the end, he was likely to have a room full of people who were deeply disappointed, raging against the injustice of having to bear the outcome of inadequate leadership.

On the other hand, he could tell them the truth and acknowledge their betrayal. He could communicate the expectation that they work as adults who could, and should, contribute to the success of the organization. This speaks to the adult nature of everyone's existence and the fact that we alone choose what we make of our future.

At least in the moment of Joe's speech, employees at this newspaper heard the message that the survival of the paper was as much in their hands as it was in senior management's. They recognized that their contributions to resolving the difficult marketplace issues in circulation, advertising, editorial, and production while managing costs would have a bearing on their futures. Rather than demanding, like children, that Joe solve the problems for them, they could choose to grow up, have hope and optimism for the future, and put their energies toward making a difference.

Learning to Grow Up

Organizations have been built on the notion that people must be held accountable and that *someone else* is in charge of doing that. This kind of thinking, more than anything else, creates and maintains parent–child conversations in the workplace that foster cultures relying on compliance rather than commitment.

The idea that we are all responsible for our own commitment is radical. It requires people to acknowledge each other as adults who are ultimately responsible for the choices they make. We must abandon the thought that others can be the source of our motivation and morale. Then new conversations must begin to engage and support that new worldview. This shift is profoundly difficult, and it is absolutely essential.

If you don't believe it, ask yourself this basic question: "What is best for this enterprise—people who are treated and behave like children, or adults who are resilient and capable of responding to difficult circumstances?" The answer is so obvious that it makes the question seem ridiculous. Yet organizations are still deeply entrenched in workplace philosophies, policies, and procedures that reinforce parent–child conversations and cultures without realizing the cost to the business.

Anyone who has worked in an organization has stories to tell about changes that were introduced in the workplace and how they failed. Even when everyone seems to be aligned and committed to a change, it only takes a few months before people start realizing, and maybe even complaining, that everything is back to "normal." The desired organizational transformation has failed to take root.

People ask what went wrong. They diagnose the situation and scratch their heads, puzzled by what caused the failure. Some blame upper management, others blame the rank and file. People point a blaming finger at the training staff or consultants. Others assert that the thinking, methods, processes, or technology were flawed or that the proper resources weren't brought to bear.

What almost always gets overlooked, however, is one of the most powerful forces in the organization. It is a force so common and so taken for granted that it is almost too obvious to see. No one thought to change the ways people see each other and the ways they talk to each other.

Change will not survive or thrive if we continue having the same conversations. Parent–child conversations and cultures are undermining our organizations' best chances for success in the marketplace. In this book, we explore the myths and traditions that have created and maintained parent–child cultures. We provide information and tools to help transform the harmful parent–child dynamic into authentic adult–adult conversations. We take a look at the importance of intentions, language, and confronting difficult issues while maintaining goodwill.

Changing the conversations has many personal and organizational ramifications. It's critical because it acknowledges the essence of individual human experience—choice. Authentic conversations honor this, and people truly become instrumental in creating a place where their work has meaning. It is also good for business. Disaffected, disengaged employees who are treated like children are not likely to be committed to customer satisfaction, use company resources wisely, or work with other departments in partnership to further business goals.

Three distinct parent–child relationship dynamics are supported and perpetuated by conversations, and we'll examine the outcomes they generate, their effect on people and culture, and the price the organization pays for their continuance.

How is language used for manipulation and effect? By focusing on our intentions and choosing different language, we explore how to create conversations that center on disclosure and engagement. We will show you ways to identify harmful conversations and the subtleties of manipulative intent, and provide outlines for generating honest, productive conversations.

While the new conversations themselves are relatively simple and straightforward, they are not for the fainthearted. Continued use of these conversations creates a world where there is no place to hide. It creates a world where we each see our responsibility and are required to take accountability for ourselves, our organizations, and the world in which we live.

Leadership implications for using conversations to change the culture are enormous and have nothing to do with the size of your office or the importance of your title. Leadership is no longer viewed as the responsibility of those with the largest offices and the best parking spots. It becomes an act of living and interacting in a way that personifies the culture you want to create while engaging others in this creation—and doing it now, in this moment. It no longer serves you to find better ways of manipulating so that you can get "them" to do something.

True leadership also means building *knowledge and literacy* instead of managing people, and anyone can do this by being as generous and distributive as possible. Today's business environment is marked by an abundance of data. We are rich in information, yet information is often hoarded in organizations as if holding it close will keep people from starving when the business fails to thrive.

Choosing authentic conversations to create an adult culture focused on personal accountability is a challenge for every single person in an organization. Were it not for risk, there would be no need for courage. The absence of courage is sleep. It is time to wake up.

The secret for sustaining successful change in organizations lies in consciously changing the nature of workplace conversations.

Chapter One

"Revolutionary Conversations for Adults"

Imagine, for a moment, working in an organization where power was distributed so widely that everyone, from the CEO to the call-center employee, understood what was at stake for the business. How would the way you talk to each other change?

In such an organization, you and everyone you worked with would have the right and the responsibility to embrace the risk in a volatile market and choose to be accountable for the whole business. By possessing organizational power, you would be responsible for maximizing your skills and competencies to contribute to greater business success. You could do the work *and* manage the work. You and your coworkers would be responsible for their own motivation and morale, for having a point of view and publicizing it with goodwill, all the while focusing on everyone's success, not just your own.

With extensive business literacy as the foundation, you could make sound decisions affecting quality, customer service, and the cycle time that affects profits without constantly dealing with layers of bureaucracy. You'd have access to resources for solving problems and be accountable for employing them wisely. With a managing strategy that values partnership, committed adults would choose to be accountable for results.

It can happen—it does happen. We saw it happen at a plant in Michigan that supplied the automotive industry with steering and suspension parts. Because product quality had deteriorated significantly at this plant, customers were threatening to pull their business. Profits were shrinking dramatically, and the plant faced a real possibility of being shut down by corporate leaders. The relationship between management and the United Auto Workers union, which represented hourly employees, was adversarial. It was clear that if something didn't change, hundreds of people would lose their jobs.

Facing this kind of pressure, the management and union teams began to see the imperative for altering the way they did business. It took time, and it was painful. It required that people see themselves and others in a different way.

Working in concert, union officials and management teams began engaging employees in new, more direct conversations. Together, they unveiled the big-picture financial statements to everyone at the plant, which illuminated the precarious state of affairs. Issues about quality were laid bare: Costs for rework and premium shipping costs were carving huge holes in the bottom line. Customers' complaints about quality and timely delivery were made public, as well as the fact that they were seeking other suppliers. High levels of overtime and absenteeism were also eroding profits. Manufacturing processes were outdated.

These realizations led to a series of new conversations about how work got done. Plant managers and union leaders came to the conclusion that the traditional assembly-line manufacturing process was inhibiting good results. Working with employees, they designed product-oriented work centers that required everyone on a team to operate all the machines and manage quality throughout the manufacturing process. Workers were charged with scheduling, taking into account the needs of their suppliers and their customers. They prepared all products for shipping. All employees were asked to greatly expand their skills and capacity.

Contract negotiations also required new conversations about the ways workers would have to change. The plant boasted about thirty job classifications, and work had been organized so that individuals were trained to perform one function of a much larger process. Through many difficult, but honest conversations throughout the contract negotiations, the classifications were reduced from thirty to three.

Work competency was redefined. Manufacturing workers trained each other, quality engineers designed and delivered training, and other workers made machine operation job aids for when individuals got stuck. Customer panels educated workers about their requirements. Former supervisors became team co-ordinators, and slowly their views of the workers evolved. This had a big effect on how they engaged workers.

People were encouraged to talk about how they felt. Some managers were openly skeptical, even cynical, that hourly employees were capable of making the changes. Some hourly employees felt betrayed by the union and wondered aloud whether labor leaders had shirked their responsibilities by agreeing to the changes and reduced job classifications. Other workers insisted that altering the way they worked was the only path to survival and advocated personal accountability. The conversations were boisterous, edgy, and often heated. They were also marked by an authenticity that had previously been lacking. Everyone was engaged in working for a solution, even if they didn't always agree on what it was.

Over the next two years, employees at the plant improved the quality of the products, regained the loyalty of their old customers, and acquired new business. The plant became one of the most profitable in the company.

This is just one story, but it is not an isolated example of what is possible. We have seen many such transformations when the values of the organization emphasize partnership and people are working for the good of the whole rather than from a self-interested perspective. Conversations change in both content and perspective when people are engaged in the workplace as adults. Employees, regardless of where they work, are far more likely to make better business decisions. Better business results spring from engaged employees who understand the interdependency necessary for success in the workplace.

Research substantiates this. Consider the following examples from the book *12: The Elements of Great Managing*, by Rodd Wagner and James K. Harter, who work for the Gallup polling organization. The book includes published results from a study based on 10 million workplace interviews, with findings such as these:

- Business units with a surplus of disengaged employees have 31 percent more turnover.

- Workgroups with very high numbers of disengaged workers lose 51 percent more of their inventory to employee theft.

- Workgroups whose engagement puts them in the bottom quartile of the Gallup database average 62 percent more accidents.

- Engaged employees average 27 percent less absenteeism.

- Being in the higher reaches of team engagement equates to 12 percent higher customer service scores than those in the bottom tier.

- Teams in the top engaged quartile are three times more likely to succeed as those in the bottom quartile, averaging 18 percent higher productivity and 12 percent higher profitability.

- In publicly traded companies, engaged organizations outperformed the earnings per share of their competitors by 18 percent and over time progressed at a faster rate than their industry peers.

According to Wagner and Harter, "The evidence is clear that the creation and maintenance of high employee engagement, as one of the few determinants of profitability largely within a company's control, is one of the most crucial imperatives of any successful organization."

The authors also include a statement that backs up the experience we had in Michigan. They say productive, creative, and profitable teams are more likely to strongly agree with the statement "I know what is expected of me at work." But that deceptively simple statement has wider ramifications, as Wagner and Harter point out: "'Knowing what's expected' is more than a job description. It is a detailed understanding of how what one person is supposed to do fits in with what everyone else is supposed to do, and how those expectations change when the circumstances change."

So what does it mean to create and maintain engagement? What is required to do this? One element of engagement is business literacy. This means ensuring that all employees know and understand the enterprise, what is needed to be successful, the marketplace stakes, and how what they do fits in with what others do. This hasn't happened in most traditional organizations, which leaves the people who have the most contact with customers the least literate about the business. They need access to the complete financial picture, including key measures of success and information about customers, suppliers, and other important players in the business. A shared vision is supported by company values, both implicit and explicit.

Engagement means understanding the story this information tells. It is the opposite of what we encountered in a conversation with Nellie, who worked at a major international insurance company where we were consulting. During introductions at a meeting, she said, "Hi, my name is Nellie, and I make charts and graphs," and then fell silent. We continued the conversation:

"That sounds interesting," we said. "What are they used for?"

"I don't really know," Nellie replied.

"Well, where does the information come from?" we asked.

"I'm not sure," she said. "It shows up in my in-box, and I make a chart or graph and put it in a folder for pickup."

Trying to get a better sense of her work, we pressed on: "How are your charts and graphs used by the company?"

She replied, "I don't really know. I just spend all day at the computer making these charts and graphs."

It was clear to us that she knew little about how what she did at her job for forty hours a week contributed to the overall success of the business. She was a pleasantly compliant employee, to be sure, but not literate about her workplace, and certainly not engaged or committed to business results. If Nellie's experience was typical, the cost to the company would be enormous.

What might be different if the routine workplace conversations at the insurance company made clear the importance of her contribution? What if Nellie understood how other departments depended on her work to make effective sales presentations, educate customers, or represent actuarial tables? If she understood how she helped make the company successful and profitable, would it facilitate unique and understanding responses for customers? Would it more likely help in the creation of knowledge and greater willingness to respond quickly to change? Would it contribute to the value of business processes?

We've long been living with a business model based on Newtonian principles that dissect the whole into parts, with the result that people in organizations are often seen as interchangeable parts in a machine. That thinking was refined during the Industrial Revolution more than one hundred years ago, which spawned the command-and-control structure that is still common today. Considering that history, it is a considerable undertaking to shift to a strategy that sees people as the complex humans they are and engages them in partnership. Distributing organizational power rather than consolidating it requires significant organizational change.

In a traditional managing strategy, which values hierarchy, compliance, and consistency, the tendency is to make the people at the top most powerful by giving them the most access to information and other resources. Those in the upper echelons see themselves as being accountable for business results and for holding others accountable.

In return for a paycheck, those being held accountable are asked to listen, obey, and trust that top leaders see things correctly and that sound decisions are being made. A major premise of Peter Block's book *The Empowered Manager*, written in 1986, is that the people in organizations who do the work are asked to comply with authority, deny self-expression, and sacrifice now for possible future rewards. His belief is that the deal for them is safety in exchange for ownership and it's a deal that is impossible to keep. We agree.

Businesses contort themselves inventing policies and procedures so that people know exactly what is allowable and what is unacceptable. Jobs are defined to the gnat's eyelash, without any context of how all the pieces fit together. Strict rules are instituted to restrict access to resources. In our work, we hear countless examples of people who have to get several levels of sign-off to spend company money. One senior director we know oversees a huge department at a high-tech company. He told us his sign-off limit is $5,000. He has responsibility for overseeing dozens of employees and maintaining complex systems that serve thousands of customers. He has always prided himself on delivering good business results, and yet he told us his experience was that "they don't trust me more than $5,000 worth."

Organizations that rely on partnership or collaboration have a different perspective. They understand that information is a kind of nourishment for the organization and that hungry people are less likely to make good decisions that serve the business. They realize that people are more likely to be accountable for things they understand. They know that combining the energies of the whole is ultimately more powerful than fostering the competitive energies that develop in a parent–child culture.

Engagement means being able to make meaningful decisions and to have the resources to act on those decisions.

Managing Strategies for Engagement

The marketplace demands results now. Your customers want attention in this moment. The necessity for flexibility and speed in the face of change is paramount. The question is how to create an organization that can:

- Quickly create and apply new knowledge

- Grant exceptions and deliver unique responses

- Foster passion and accountability throughout the entire enterprise

For these significant changes to occur, three areas in the organization must be affected: (1) culture and management/governance practices, (2) architecture, which includes the ways jobs are designed and how people are grouped, and (3) the ways in which employees are rewarded. For all these changes to be planted and take root, new conversations are required.

Individuals must accept personal accountability for the success of the whole business and be responsible for their own motivation and morale. The culture must generate passion for the work and action in service of customers and good results. This requires less focus on personal ambition and a sincere commitment to the success of others.

Organizations have to create and sustain universal business literacy and adult-to-adult conversations, one person at a time. Management practices, such as budgeting, meetings, training, objective setting, performance reviews, and so on, must be recreated to encourage partnership. Dissent must be viewed as healthy. Through different conversations, knowledge and collaboration are baked into the work process, replacing compliance and control as the operating values.

Where to start? If the longest journey begins with a single step, it won't surprise you that our advice is to begin by changing the conversations. Better conversations will reap rich, diverse information. They will encourage an examination of who plays key roles in improving business results. They will allow you to address difficult issues in a constructive way.

New conversations will champion the kind of learning and resourcefulness that lead to innovation, cost efficiencies, and personal accountability—essential elements in addressing the complex problems of organizational renovation.

Chapter Two

" Relationships That Don't Work at Work "

Most organizations operate with a cultural dynamic that is as familiar as it is difficult and unproductive. Familiar because we have all experienced it in some way or another within the context of our families. Difficult because in today's demanding business environment, an entrenched parent–child culture in the workplace won't lead to the best results.

Reams have been written about parent–child cultures in the context of organizations and the workplace. For those interested in learning more, we encourage an exploration of the writings of Eric Berne and Thomas Anthony Harris. For our purpose here, the idea isn't so much that management represents parents and employees are the children. Rather, we are talking about the conversational roles used routinely in the workplace that establish and reinforce parent–child cultures. If organizations don't find a way to shift to an adult–adult culture, they will be ill equipped to survive in the highly technical, global, diverse, and changing-at-the-speed-of-light marketplace.

If new conversations are to initiate true cultural change, it is essential to understand how conversations perpetuate a parent–child culture. Such parent–child conversations send and underscore a message that compliance is valued over commitment, control over creativity, and predictability over innovation. In more than twenty years of doing work with organizations, we have found that these dysfunctional workplace conversations usually can be categorized under three general themes:

- **Holding others accountable:** "It is critical to roll out this new policy carefully so that people will get on board with it. We have to make sure they get it and do it right."

- **Caretaking:** "Things might look a little shaky right now, but just ignore the rumors and do the best job you can. Everything will be fine."

- **Coping with disappointment and colluding with cynicism:** "Did you hear about the latest change they want to make? It will never work. When will they realize that no one ever takes this stuff seriously?"

In all cases, these types of conversations have a detrimental impact on the culture and the business. They send erroneous messages that people don't choose their own level of accountability and assume that someone else can do it for them. They let employees off the hook for being honest and responsible for business results. They allow individuals to avoid difficult issues and discourage them from using their initiative and resources for solving problems. And they derail change initiatives and innovations because people aren't confronted when they won't let go of past disappointments or failures. The assumption inherent in all these conversations is that people can't be treated—or talked to—like the adults they are, and that "children" must adhere to "parental" authority.

Historically, organizations have been built around the belief that people won't work unless they are constantly watched. This idea was perfected during the Industrial Revolution as management layers were created to watch workers and make sure they were (1) doing the work and (2) not messing with the work. Using a parent–child analogy, Johnny and Sally will refuse to behave properly or contribute to the household unless their parents constantly supervise them, promise them an allowance, or threaten them with punishment.

Children exchange their freedom and self-expression for shelter, food, and security. It makes sense with small children in a family, because children can't survive on their own and have to be taught certain skills to be able to live independently. But does a similar system make sense in an organization populated by intelligent grown-ups capable of making good decisions? After all, these same individuals live complex lives outside of work and usually manage just fine.

Whom do you want showing up at work? Children who need a long list of rules and regulations and constant oversight to be held accountable? Or grown-ups who are able to, and choose to, hold themselves accountable?

Holding Others Accountable

Organizations can't function without accountability, and we are not contending that accountability isn't vital to the success of any endeavor. In a business environment that is fast, mean, and asks more from each of us than at any time in history, accountability is absolutely essential.

"Holding others accountable" is a phrase so common people don't stop to think about its real meaning. The way employees see and talk about accountability is a critical issue in the workplace, and the notion of holding others accountable has unintended consequences. Myriad management practices and policies have been designed to hold others accountable, and huge resources are continually devoted to finding better ways to accomplish this impossible task. Requiring employees to punch a time clock is one example; another is submitting weekly activity logs to managers. Yearly performance evaluations are a time when bosses "make sure" that workers are held accountable for the quality of their work.

Tough, results-oriented managers who have been good at holding people accountable are praised and promoted, and enormous amounts of their time are spent making sure other people get things done. Organizational charts are developed and published so that it's apparent who answers to whom for which results. The message of these policies and practices is clear: "If someone else weren't holding you accountable, this place would fall apart."

When we consult with organizations, one of the first things we do is interview people to get a feel for how things work and what employees' perceptions are. One question we always ask is "Who is accountable and responsible for the success of the business?"

Inevitably, the core worker will say "my boss" or "management" or "the CEO." Often he or she responds with two words and a gesture: "They are!" with index finger always pointing upward.

So we go up, both literally and figuratively, in search of "Them." We ask upper management, "Who is accountable and responsible for the success of the business?" And they tell us "workers" or "the employees." It is management's job to plan, to worry, and to make sure, but the workers who serve customers are responsible for success. Management, too, often responds with two words and a gesture: "They are," index finger always pointing downward.

Here's the conundrum: Using the frame of "holding others accountable" has created cultures where nobody owns responsibility or takes accountability for the success of the business. When management focuses so much attention on holding others accountable, they are actually making them less accountable. Workers aren't necessarily choosing accountability; they're just accepting that someone else is going to hold them accountable. Under this system, people become responsible only for the limited scope of their jobs or roles and are not typically encouraged to be concerned with how they affect others or the big picture.

How might an organization's success in the marketplace be influenced if everyone involved in the enterprise answered the question "Who is accountable and responsible?" with a sincere and resounding "I am!" and then acted like it?

Caretaking and Reassurance

When dealing with young children, it makes sense to shield and protect them from some of the world's harsh realities. But how does that translate to adults in an organization trying to survive in a highly competitive business environment?

It is irresponsible and counterproductive to withhold information that employees require to help the business survive. An ever-changing marketplace *demands* that workers make changes in their performance and in what they contribute to the business. They need to be prepared for doing this, but why would they prepare when they're consistently being told, "Don't worry. We'll take care of it," or "Just focus on doing your job and let us worry about the big picture."

One example of organizational caretaking is reflected in the use of employee attitude assessment surveys. Senior management or the human resources department typically commissions these surveys to assess the health of an organization or to discover problems with morale. Employees are allowed to remain anonymous to "protect them" from possible consequences.

Employees also get the message that it is someone else's responsibility to do something about the problems they see. A more subtle form of caretaking is that the survey's anonymity allows employees to say whatever they want without being accountable for it. They are off the hook. This parent–child exercise of attitude assessments is a profound cultural statement that it's not safe to tell the truth at work and own it.

Caretaking implies that managers are more accountable for the organization than core workers. When you try to manage people's feelings toward organizational change, you are telling them they are not responsible for their own responses to change. It doesn't serve anyone to create a false sense of security or to send a message, however subtle, that "you can't handle the truth." This helps create victims, helpless people who are primed for a justified sense of outrage and betrayal if things don't turn out all right.

Workers who demand reassurance are equally responsible for this dangerous dynamic. No one can predict the future. Jobs are never secure. Workers reinforce the parent–child culture and attempt to absolve themselves of responsibility for the organization's future by retreating into the childlike stance of "Just take care of me, I don't want to worry. I want to be able to blame someone else when things go wrong."

Disappointment and Cynicism

Cynicism is an unproductive reaction to disappointment. It springs from the helplessness people feel when they are disappointed by others, and allows them to become detached observers rather than active participants. It carries with it a sense of entitlement: "You have disappointed me, therefore my cynicism is justified." Cynics have enormous data to support their positions. History is always on their side. In effect, they are telling their organizations, "Don't try to tell me things are going to get better, because I have been here long enough to know that they won't. You will just disappoint me again."

Cynicism breeds harmful negativity. Organizations frequently present it as a morale problem, a failure of employees to "get on board" or "develop a positive attitude." This also reinforces the parent–child dynamic. Think about what happens when a child takes a harmless tumble and her parents respond to her wails with "Stop crying. You are not really hurt." The child usually begins howling louder to prove them wrong. When was the last time you told your child to "lose the attitude" and he responded with a bright smile and sudden enthusiasm for the task at hand?

The same thing happens when the organizational response to cynicism is to soft-pedal the cynic's experience of disappointment. This is exacerbated when the solution to combat cynicism is to sell, barter, or make promises to the cynic in an effort to enlist future commitment and optimism. Even worse is a demand to banish cynicism. How often have managers been told they must get their employees on board with a company initiative? How often do employees blame low morale on their managers and expect them to do something about it, as if someone else could be in charge of their perspectives or motivation?

The bartering conversation goes something like this: "I know you're upset by how things have been going around here and a lot of what you've been saying is true. But it's going to be different now. We're making changes and senior management is really behind them this time. I really believe our unit is going to get the support it needs. You can be an important part of its success, but you have to let go of the negative and accentuate the positive." Sometimes it isn't couched quite so kindly: "This change is going to happen with or without you, so I suggest you change your attitude."

Cynics view this skeptically at best. As one employee was overheard to remark, "These situations remind me of what my parents used to say to me."

Promising is another form of selling or bartering. For example, an attitude survey indicates employees are blaming poor morale on the fact that senior management is uninterested in their opinions. The typical reaction? Managers stage a series of meetings where they promise employees that they will do things differently. "We promise to listen better, to communicate more clearly. We'll put in a suggestion box! And we'll implement great new programs to ensure that everyone is treated fairly." Isn't it interesting that the employees who respond to those surveys are never asked to account for their contributions to poor morale?

These conversations ask people for their commitment and optimism in exchange for assurances they won't be disappointed down the road. It's an impossible deal. The cynic knows it, and so do you. The workplace is littered with stories of change efforts that have failed, management teams that have come and gone, projects that were started and then abandoned, procedures that promised true reform but fizzled after a few months.

If building an organization where people choose accountability for themselves and accountability for the business is the true desire, conversations must change.

A New View of People and Work

Changing the conversations means you must first change your assumptions about people, who they are, and what they can handle. It means redefining who is accountable and what it means to lead.

People at work in traditional organizations are often viewed as objects, parts in a process to be rearranged. They are seen as having behaviors that must be managed. They are seen as "not getting it." And they are seen as needing benevolent authority in order to function properly.

Changing conversations means seeing people for who they really are. Everyone brings legitimate points of views about their circumstances. Everyone chooses behaviors they consider appropriate and effective in any given situation. People create visions of a future that has meaning for them. The first question people ask themselves when things change is "How does this affect me?" Everyone is always choosing whether to approach the world with a desire to create worth, with an overall sense of disappointment, or by trying to get ahead at all costs. If we find ourselves denying these things about another person, we must be willing to deny these things about ourselves.

The table on the next page lists traditional assumptions about people and work and offers new assumptions you might make instead.

In the next three chapters, we'll go deeper into dysfunctional conversations, exploring a little organizational history and giving you specific examples of what the dangerous conversations sound like and the negative business impact they can have.

In later chapters, we'll show how changing the conversation can begin to build a culture of accountability and support lasting change. We'll give you practical ways to start having new conversations.

Old Assumptions	New Assumptions
Seeing people as objects	Seeing people as complex human beings
Viewing people's feelings about their individual experiences as useless and irrelevant in creating the future	Inviting and encouraging the disclosure of individual plans and feelings in creating a shared future
Ignoring the freedom and will of the individual	Emphasizing freedom and accountability of the individual
Seeking techniques to shape behavior and manage emotional responses	Framing choices as the primary means for engagement and creating change
Using policies, procedures, and practices to ensure compliance and alignment	Using policies, procedures, and practices to encourage engagement, disclosure, and commitment
Having faith in leadership, experts, and authority to make things happen	Having faith in collaboration, goodwill, and intelligence to make things happen
Insisting that the dominant and relevant reality is:	Acknowledging the primary reality is the experience of the person and his or her:
• Roles and responsibilities	• Plans
• Job descriptions	• Projects
• Practices	• Concerns
• Procedures	• Sense of meaing
• Processes	• Practical motives
• Structures	• Behavior
• Coprorate visions and values	• Way he or she sees things

Chapter Three

"The Myth of Holding Others Accountable "

Let's get this on the table right away. The notion that you can hold other people accountable is a myth, a dangerous illusion that denies a fundamental reality of human existence. People *always* have a choice about their beliefs and actions. You choose to be accountable—it can't be forced upon you. When you continue to have conversations about holding others accountable, you are only perpetuating the myth and the parent–child dynamic.

Several years ago, we were working with senior management in a large clothing manufacturing company. This company was making business changes under a very difficult set of marketplace circumstances. They were doing what management teams often do in these situations: cutting expenses, reducing payroll, rearranging structures, reengineering processes, and searching for techniques to manage the diverse constituencies that would be affected.

Preliminary meetings where several of the changes were introduced had not gone particularly well. The news was bad and people were upset. Senior managers had done the best they could to cajole, reassure, and promise employees that they should get on board with the changes for the good of the company. Soon after, a senior executive received an anonymous memo:

TO: The Senior Management Team

SUBJECT: Some thoughts on your change effort

Before you conceive of ways to understand me, before you name me anything, I find myself with choices to make and a future to create. Before I am a name or number, an employee, a part of the process or system or a manager—before I am anything you may say about me—*I am here deciding what to make of my life.*

I decide what to make of you and your plans for me. I decide what meaning you will have in my life. I will decide for myself the future I want to pursue and the place you have in it. Deciding these things is not in your hands. *You cannot demand my commitment, my passion or even determine my destiny. I choose or reject these things for my own reasons.* [Emphasis added.]

The memo articulates beautifully the dilemma faced by organizations that focus on holding people accountable. People always decide for themselves what to make of the circumstances and the demands that are being made of them. There are three possible scenarios:

You choose commitment. You internalize the choice and consistently make decisions that live out that commitment. You show up with passion, enthusiasm, and energy. Your mindset is focused on doing excellent work and having honest conversations. Motivation is *intrinsic* as you focus on resolving dilemmas, finding creative solutions, contributing worth, and continually improving business results. You are accountable because you choose to be, not because of someone else's perceived authority.

You choose compliance. The focus is on the consequences of not being accountable. You do what you are told because you like your boss or fear her or his authority. You fear risking the relationship, your paycheck, or both. You may even believe that compliance, rather than commitment, is what is expected. (And that may be right.) What you are asked to do may not even make sense to you, but you don't challenge it for fear of being labeled "uncooperative" or "not a team player." Motivation is *extrinsic*, and the driving values are doing what you are told, maintaining relationships, doing acceptable work, getting a good review and a raise, and, at the most extreme end of the spectrum, not getting fired. Your conversations are practical, transactional, and focused on the job at hand.

You choose the appearance of compliance. The focus is on appearing to be accountable while skating as close to the edge of noncompliance as possible. Your driving forces are fear, frustration, and/or anger. What you are asked to do often makes no sense to you, so you vent frustration by directing your energy into finding "work-arounds" and/or sabotaging initiatives. Time is spent enlisting coworkers to join in your cynicism. You don't participate in outright insubordination, but conversations are focused on making sure everyone around you understands everything that is wrong with the workplace rather than using your energies to find creative solutions to problems.

In all cases, *you* make these choices.

Consider another parent–child analogy. Parents who try to hold their children accountable for homework are likely to see one of three things happen, just as in the examples above. In the first scenario, Sally internalizes the commitment to learning and pours her passions into completing assignments, doing homework, cooperating with fellow students and the teacher. She mines every opportunity for discovering knowledge. Her parents soon realize they don't need to make sure Sally is a good student because she is committed to learning and doing well in school.

In the second scenario, Sally chooses to comply with parental authority because she doesn't want to face the consequences that come with getting bad grades. She does her homework because she worries about losing privileges or because she fears her parents won't love her if she isn't a good student. She puts in just enough effort to get by, but without her parents' constant reminders and occasional threats, the first priority for her energies is to play video games and chat online with her friends.

In the final scenario, Sally finds any excuse she can to avoid doing her work. She consistently "forgets" to bring homework home or lies to her parents about having assignments. When her parents get tough and stand over her until she gets her work done, she loses it on the way to school. If she's old enough, maybe she doesn't show up at all. Or she does homework to escape immediate consequences, but sabotages her progress at school by fighting with classmates, disrespecting her teacher, or daydreaming in class. In all of these scenarios, Sally makes her choices regardless of what her parents say or do.

Think about your own life. How does your attitude toward the things you do because you must comply (paying household bills and taxes, cleaning or maintaining your home, registering your car, and so forth) differ from your attitude toward what you are committed to (your family, a loved one, your church, a cause for which you have passion)? It's the difference between the person who jogs because he's afraid of getting fat and the person who trains for a marathon. The jogger gets it over with; the marathon runner is fueled by passion and commitment.

Compliance and Control

More than one hundred years of organizational history have worked to reinforce the myth that others have an ability and responsibility for enforcing accountability. Since the Industrial Revolution, we have built organizations with a prevailing philosophy that adults won't choose accountability on their own and so they must be bribed or coerced. Organizations have spent enormous energy and resources hammering home the message that someone else will be responsible for your accountability, the subtext being that you are absolved from that obligation.

Frederick Winslow Taylor, often called the father of scientific management theory, was among the first to develop and fine-tune this philosophy. He was instrumental in devising systems that organized chaotic shop floors and maximized the interaction between man and machine. Taylor's system was based on a cynical view of how human beings would behave if someone didn't force them to work. In his words, "hardly a competent workman can be found who does not devote a considerable part of his time to studying just how slowly he can work and still convince his employer that he is going at a good pace."

Taylor espoused the idea that the "first class man"—he who was better and more efficient at performing a task—should be appointed to watch other workers. These "first class men" were given the responsibility to design and organize the work and to make sure plans were followed. This established a hierarchy where one person does the work and another is responsible for making sure the work gets done. Even today, a key role of management responsibility is to "make sure" and hold people accountable.

That kind of thinking and the organizational systems constructed around it have contributed heavily to today's parent–child culture in the workplace. Charts are created so that people are clear about how the system works and who is in charge. Parent–child performance review systems and compensation that is tied to performance make sure people get the message. Over time, organizations have become more benevolent about holding people accountable. For example, posters are displayed touting "people are our most important resource," and supervisors are trained to give feedback in more humane ways. Even so, workplace conversations have an abundance of parent–child messages that say "we don't think you can choose to be accountable, so we are going to make sure you are." We have built cultures of compliance believing that was enough, and for nearly a century, we have achieved success.

The question bears repeating: How much greater are our chances of success if we create cultures where people choose commitment for the good of the whole? Where our conversations about holding others accountable are transformed to conversations about individual commitment and the ways we hold ourselves accountable?

This issue is illustrated in work we did with a medical claims unit in a major health care company. The department was getting tremendous heat for its poor performance from corporate headquarters, medical care providers, and customers. Management teams had come and gone, new processes and procedures had been instituted. Still the workers who processed claims consistently missed their targets, and the number of unprocessed claims remained unacceptably high. In addition, after three failed audits, Medicare had threatened to yank its business, which comprised about 60 percent of the department's revenue.

Soon after we began working there, a new director was brought in. Her first responses seemed to spark improvements. She offered overtime-pay incentives, cajoled, provided free food, held pep rallies and contests. The number of unprocessed claims began to drop. Corporate leaders gave the department an exemption for improving results while she hired new processors to ease the workload. After the new hires were trained and in place, most of the incentives and increased overtime opportunities were withdrawn. The number of unprocessed claims started climbing again. At staff meetings, the director emphatically told employees that corporate would no longer tolerate the high claims inventory. Her feet were being held to the fire on this issue. "Even if I lose my job over this," she told them, "someone else will come in to deliver the same message."

Employees generally shrugged. They had heard these messages numerous times before from previous management teams. Those managers were gone, and the claims processors were still there.

As pressure mounted, the director decided that supervisors weren't doing enough to make sure the work got done. Without discussing it with them, she decided supervisors should give up their offices and start working from cubicles on the floor to keep a better eye on the employees who were not meeting quotas. Supervisors were expected to get serious about corrective action for poor performance. Unless employees showed improvement, the corrective action would eventually lead to employees being fired. About this time, several employees filed grievances with the labor union, which heightened the tension.

And still the numbers remained unacceptably high. For years, employees had been receiving the message to focus on their work and let management focus on solving problems. But the problems and solutions that management came up with were inextricably tied to the work done by employees. Claims processors were frustrated by having little or no voice in how things might turn out. The complaint we often heard from them was "Why won't they treat us like adults and let us have a say in our future?" Management's reply was "We'll treat them like adults when they start acting like adults by being responsible and getting the work done." A classic parent–child stalemate. While they indulged in this circular argument, the business was suffering and the department's future was in jeopardy. Based on nothing but the cold, hard numbers, it would have made more sense for the health care company to outsource the work of the claims department rather than to continue subsidizing nonperformance.

To be fair, other factors complicated this scenario: deep-seated resentments, old disputes between labor and management, outdated equipment and technology. Even so, the director and managers exhausted themselves trying to hold other people accountable. Frustrated, resentful employees consistently chose compliance or the appearance of compliance over commitment to resolving a very real business crisis. As with many organizations, the well-established parent–child conversations had created a culture where people focused more on their own agendas than doing what was best for the business. Neither side found the will to change this debilitating dynamic.

Parent–child conversations and cultures are so much a part of our organizational environment that we don't even see them, in the same way fish don't see the water in which they live. Jim Laub, a professor at Indiana Wesleyan University, did research supporting this assertion. Laub used an instrument called the Organizational Leadership Assessment to determine whether perceptions of an organization's health were consistent throughout the organization. According to his findings, most workers experience leadership within their organization as "paternalistic," defined as a benevolent rule that has the effect of producing childlike responses in followers. Laub writes that paternalistic leaders see themselves as parents. They put the needs of the organization first and treat workers as children. "Those led accept that the leaders know more, are wiser, and that the led must simply follow, even if it means abdicating their own responsibility to lead."

In essence, Laub's research characterizes parent–child cultures as unhealthy for "any organization that desires to develop leadership throughout the organization, empower others to act and build a community of capable partners to fulfill an agreed-upon mission and vision." Healthy adult–adult cultures are characterized as places "where people serve the interests of others, above their own self interest, for the good of the organization as a whole."

Laub's research also shows that leaders in paternalistic cultures consistently tend to view their organizations as more healthy than the workers view it. This difference in perception perpetuates an "us and them" mentality that works against true community. In organizations that have adult–adult cultures, Laub's research finds that views on the overall health of the organization are more closely aligned among management and workers.

A managing strategy that puts compliance as its primary value creates paternalistic cultures. Such cultures don't exist when people see each other as peers, associates, or collaborators. When one group, typically employees, is consistently asked to yield to another, typically managers, it's only natural that each group has a different perspective on the organization's health. Addressing these conflicting perspectives means calling into question compliance as a managing value.

The essential first step for change is recognizing that compliance is the best result we are likely to get from strategies and systems focused on holding others accountable. Business leaders must ask themselves, "Is compliance enough for success?" If the answer is no, then it is critical to choose strategies that call for engagement and personal accountability. Learning new conversations to talk about these issues is imperative. When we learn to recognize each other as adults who make choices about accountability and talk to each other in a different way, we can begin to transform the culture's focus from watching to doing.

Organizations that have improved their businesses by creating cultures of accountability often talk about the importance of adulthood. Over several years, Ricardo Semler transformed his Brazilian company, Semco, from a hierarchal, command-and-control structure to one where workers see themselves as much responsible for Semco's success as the CEO. Workers design their own workspaces, decide how products are manufactured, and, in many cases, set their own salaries. Semler even involves employees in choosing the location of new plants. Semco has thrived in a tough environment while contending with strong unions, corrupt governments, and a wildly fluctuating economy. The company, which employed ninety people in 1982 with revenues of $4 million, grew to 3,000 employees and boasted revenues of $212 million by 2003, with an employee turnover rate of about 1 percent. Semler's explanation of this achievement: "It's all very simple. All we are doing is treating people like adults." (For a glimpse of what's possible, we highly recommend his books *Maverick!* and *The Seven-Day Weekend: Changing the Way Work Works.*)

A similar example is seen at the Chaparral Steel Company, based in Midlothian, Texas. Gordon E. Forward, former vice chairman of Texas Industries Inc., was president and CEO of Chaparral Steel, which in 1992 had the distinction of being the lowest-cost steel producer in the world. According to a profile in *Fortune* magazine, his espoused management philosophy was a classless corporation, universal education, and freedom to act, where top managers "treat workers like adults." "Real motivation comes from within," Forward was quoted in the article. "People have to be given the freedom to succeed or fail." He jokingly called his personal style "management by adultery."

Clarity of personal belief and intention is a critical first act toward changing culture, but personal clarity isn't enough. Accountability demands honesty and visibility, especially in organizations. People need to know where you stand so they know if they can count on you. Honest conversations between adults confront doubts and fears about the future and help assess the risks they are willing to take together. We all have doubts about the future and about ourselves. We just haven't considered these doubts to be appropriate business talk. Instead, we have covered up our concerns with positive spin and speeches about the importance of holding others accountable.

As adults, we can begin making promises we intend to keep. We can talk about the results we are willing to be accountable for. We can create space for collaboration, dissent, honest feedback, and critique. We can negotiate honorably and begin speaking *together* as the voice of the business. We can choose our own consequences when we fail to deliver in order to publicly signal our seriousness about honoring the commitments we make. We choose to do this for the community and ourselves, not because our parents said so.

Upcoming chapters give voice to these new conversations by providing structures and sample outlines that are useful for changing the parent–child dynamic. The first step is to recognize each other as adults with choices to make and futures to create.

Chapter Four

" You Can't Make All the Fourth Graders Happy "

When Jamie's son, Zak, was ten years old, the two of them took a soccer road trip along with Zak's friend Luke. They were chatting over a fast-food lunch when Luke suddenly made an important announcement. "Hey, did I tell you," he said excitedly, "that I was elected as the fourth-grade class executive?"

Zak was impressed. "Man, you're lucky. We don't even have class executives."

Jamie was curious. "So tell me, Luke, what exactly does the fourth-grade class executive do? Do you run the fourth grade?"

Luke shook his head. "I don't really run the fourth grade. My job is to go to dances and other school events and make sure all the fourth graders are happy."

Jamie could do nothing but laugh at Luke's job description of an executive. At age ten, Luke saw his job as being as responsible for the happiness of the entire fourth grade. We do start 'em young.

This is a humorous illustration of the difficulty created by workplace conversations that center on caretaking. It shows how ludicrous the idea of one person being responsible for another's emotional welfare really is.

When talking about authentic conversations, we make a distinction between "taking care" of people and "caretaking" of people. Taking care of others is born of kindness, compassion, and empathy. It manifests itself in goodwill and considering others' viewpoints. It is what you do for your children when they're sick or because they're too young to take care of themselves. You take care of your friends when they are hurting and need a listening ear, and you take care of your neighbors when they are in a jam. This is different from caretaking, which we define as trying to manage (or be responsible for) another's emotional response to a given situation or set of circumstances.

When you cross the line of compassion and concern and attempt to take responsibility for someone else's emotional response, the impulse to protect ends up harming instead. When clans of people lived in caves and one of them discovered a tiger's lair close by, he or she was probably frightened. But the answer to protecting the clan wasn't to withhold the location of the cave so the others wouldn't be frightened, or to downplay the possibility of a hungry tiger attacking them. Acknowledging the fearful circumstances and using the clan's collective wisdom to find a practical solution is not only more pragmatic, it could be essential to survival.

To think that you can manage another's emotional welfare is a dangerous game and requires willful dishonesty. Sometimes we deceive ourselves into thinking that caretaking is about compassion, about protecting someone "for their own good," when the truth is we don't want to deal with the emotional fallout that usually accompanies difficult news and challenging choices. If someone asks for the truth, and you tell him what you think he wants to hear, you have deceived him. That kind of deception is a demeaning and debilitating message to the adults we work with, those we have asked to show up each day and contribute their best.

Caretaking conversations are routine in traditional organizations. They have the unintended consequences of creating cultures where people do not see themselves as responsible for their own emotional welfare or as players who have a critical role in the organization's success and survival. It is yet another manifestation of the parent–child dynamic.

One of the hardest things for parents to acknowledge is our inability to protect our children from the world's harsh realities. It also stands to reason that the harder we try to protect them, shield them from difficult issues, and reassure them that everything will turn out all right, the less likely they are to grow up and figure out how to manage a tricky world on their own.

Caretaking in Conversations

The caretaking dynamic shows up in two types of workplace conversations: *reassuring/protecting* and *prescribing/directing*. By their very nature, these conversations are inauthentic and will lead to betrayal and disappointment. Such conversations actually deflect people's attention and energy away from solving the real business issues.

Traditional models of strong leadership have rewarded these kinds of conversations, creating cultures where we expect our leaders to provide answers, exude confidence, and keep doubts about the future to themselves. Leaders use reassuring conversations to demonstrate how seriously they take their responsibilities both for solving problems and providing protection and certainty for those in their care. "You don't have to worry about anything. Just focus on getting your work done. As your leaders, we promise you that we are busy solving these serious problems so that everything will work out."

Employees collude with this parent–child dynamic by striking this bargain: "I will give you my loyalty and commitment in exchange for the reassurance and certainty that you provide me about the future." They buy the message that it is not really their job to be responsible for their own future or the success of the business.

These conversations are powerful and appealing. Listeners hear what they want to hear—that someone else will take charge of their safety and security. What a seductive promise! At some level, many of us would prefer to believe our survival is in the hands of someone or something else. Even if it's a false security, it takes the edge off and helps us sleep at night. And in its most extreme form, it absolves us from all blame.

During the Bush/Clinton presidential campaign debate, President George H. W. Bush was asked, "What is your vision for America?" He dismissively answered, "Oh, the vision thing." People were bothered by his answer, and some pundits attributed that moment as the beginning of the end of his reelection hopes. People want a president with a sense of vision and someone who offers them (or almost guarantees) the emotional security they long for. These days it's tough to get elected if you can't promise to keep people safe. But there isn't a leader in the world who can promise that future. Leaders can promise to hold themselves accountable for specific results, they can promise to work as hard as they can to achieve them, and they can promise to keep their word.

But they can't keep a promise to make all the fourth graders happy.

"Everything Will Be Okay"

One manager we were working with recently turned to us for advice. "Our unit is being redefined and redesigned, and all the jobs are changing," he said. "No one knows where we are going to land, and they're all coming to me. They know there are going to be fewer jobs, but they don't know who is going to survive the cut. What the heck do I say to them?"

We asked him, "What have you been saying?" He told us he was protecting them as best he could, assuring them that things would turn out all right. "I usually say things like, 'Just do your job. Do the best you can today and don't worry about the rest.'" This is not a useful conversation. It was clear some employees were going to get reassigned or lose their jobs, and it was unlikely that things would turn out all right for everybody. His reassurances (however well intended) wouldn't help workers deal with the fact that their jobs were at risk. His attempts to protect them would not help them prepare for the future.

This manager was competent, caring, and compassionate. He had good intentions. But caretaking is a form of control. He might have thought he was being kind and helpful, but attempting to manage someone's emotional response is neither kind nor compassionate.

In circumstances that are challenging and difficult, if you tell others not to worry, that everything is under control and it will be all right, your intention is to get a specific emotional response. In essence, you are attempting to deny someone else the opportunity to respond as he or she chooses. The hope is that you can stop others from feeling fearful or worried or angry. By turning away from those emotions, they will be free to focus and pour their energies into doing the job—or at least stop pestering you with their worries so that you can work.

If you get the response you are trying to evoke, you may see it as an affirmation that caretaking works. You believe you have changed the way the other feels and lose sight of the fact that he or she *made a choice* to feel reassured—even in the face of contradictory data.

A caretaking response almost always involves delivering partial information or false information. If someone chooses to feel reassured and hopeful based on your reassurances, which are based on a false reality, you have set him or her up for a deep sense of betrayal, disappointment, and anger if things don't turn out all right. None of us can make promises about the future, especially in difficult, challenging times. But you can choose to be forthright about the circumstances as you know them.

Caretaking sends a message, intended or not, that people aren't responsible for creating their own futures and looking for ways to solve problems. Even if things do work out, another brick has been added to the wall of childish behavior. On the inevitable day when things don't turn out fine, that wall is going to crumble, leaving everyone in a pile of emotional rubble because they chose false security over preparing for a real future.

In today's demanding and uncertain world, it makes sense for people to focus on what is needed to build the capacity of the business rather than how to protect one another. It is a radical and essential change to have conversations that frame choices for people and remind them of their responsibility in creating a preferred future. By doing this consistently, we can begin to abandon parent–child roles and create adult cultures where people know and understand that they are responsible for their emotional responses.

"Let Me Tell You What to Do . . ."

Prescribing and directing are forms of caretaking that tend to be more aggressive and confronting. Managers take on the role of authoritarian, omniscient parent and make sure employees know that, as managers, it is their job to be in control and to provide the answers. Their energy is focused on telling people what the desired outcomes are and exactly how to achieve them. They provide the remedies when problematic situations arise. Traditional business cultures have rewarded managers for this behavior. But something very real is lost when a large part of the workforce isn't invited to participate.

We were talking with the director of a highly regarded charter school in the southwestern United States, whose goal was to franchise her education model nationally and internationally. She talked to us about her frustration over her lack of time for focusing on planning and business strategies. "Everyone complains if I'm not available to answer questions and solve problems," she said. "They need me to give direction and tell them what to do."

When asked why she couldn't rely on her employees to solve their own problems within the framework of the school's goals, she vigorously shook her head. "No, no. I don't *want* them doing that. They might make the wrong decisions. They don't know everything I do, so I need to know what's going on and then tell them how to handle it. This place needs that control."

Even if she found time to plan for the future and focus on strategies, we suggested, she would have a hard time achieving her objectives if she didn't start building the capacity of her employees. She had hired a staff of bright, capable, hardworking people. Yet her conversations sent the message that she didn't trust them to know what she knew so they could figure things out for themselves. She was telling them, "Let me do the thinking. You just act on my decisions." She was, in effect, using them as a "pair of hands" to carry out her wishes.

Her eyes widened. She didn't want to send them that message at all, she told us, and she definitely wanted to build a staff that was creative, involved, and self-reliant. She just wasn't sure how to let go of the reins and let people solve their own problems. She wanted to be a resource for them if they needed her, but she also wanted to be kept in the loop so that the school's mission remained intact.

Here again was a bright, competent, caring individual with good intentions for the business. Yet she wasn't aware that her conversations with employees were contributing heavily to the very difficulty she was talking about. By prescribing and directing, she was sending the message that she wanted control, and her employees felt powerless to act without her knowledge and permission. The staff was dedicated and felt a responsibility for creating a successful enterprise, but they had developed the dangerous habit of waiting to be told what to do rather than seeking out solutions for themselves.

When a few people are seen as being responsible for providing answers for the many, myriad possibilities and creative solutions are overlooked and go unexplored. Organizations where only a handful of people at the top see themselves as responsible for business results are wasting huge amounts of important information and experience contained in the other people working in the organization. Often these are the very people who are closest to the core work and the customers they serve. It is difficult to understand why organizations wouldn't want as many capable adults as possible focused on serving customers, resolving business issues, and looking for the best ways to survive in today's demanding, unforgiving marketplace.

Betrayal and Disappointment

Whenever you engage in conversations that are reassuring/protecting or prescribing/directing, you do one or more of these four things:

- Reinforce the notion that everyone's survival is in the leaders' hands
- Attempt to control the reactions of others with partial or false information
- Establish a mindset that leaders are more capable and accountable for creating the world
- Set up others to feel betrayed and disappointed

Consider this hypothetical but realistic example. The CEO of a large company is fighting with members of the board over cutting costs. He passionately outlines to them why he thinks this will hurt the business. He even manages to persuade board members to adjust their expectations and in doing so saves hundreds of jobs. Even so, layoffs and reassignments are required.

While all this is going on, top managers send consistent messages to employees that they are looking for solutions to business problems. When layoff announcements are made, employees feel betrayed. They are angry and hostile because the message they have been hearing is "Don't worry, we are going to solve these problems for you so it turns out okay." It was a promise that couldn't be kept. The betrayal is real and natural.

Employees fail to see that they have colluded with the caretaking by naively believing that everything would be okay. Their experience in the moment is that they have been lied to. Those who were laid off are gone, and those who remain see management's "betrayal" as righteous justification for their cynicism and lack of commitment.

Leaders also feel betrayed and disappointed. "How could they react so ungratefully after all we have done for them? We fought with the board. We saved jobs. We put everything we could into turning this situation around." This feeling of betrayal is also real and natural. The leaders' efforts were done with good intentions to make things turn out all right for everyone. As each howls about the betrayal of the other, the business of the business is jeopardized, in the moment and going forward.

Whether you intend to or not, you make hostages of those you try to caretake. Hostages are people whose experience is that they have no choice about their situation. Sometimes caretaking is selfish—done in the name of protecting the business: "If we tell them how bad it is, they won't be able to do their jobs or they might find new jobs and leave us high and dry." Sometimes it is done because you are trying to ease people's emotions. And often, the painful truth is you just don't want to deal with the unpleasantness that might be contained in the reactions of others. You tell yourself, "They can't handle the truth" when in reality you have a deep reluctance to entertain someone else's emotional fallout from the truth.

Any way you look at it, when you caretake others they become your hostages, and hostage situations usually end well only in the movies.

For new conversations to begin, leaders and employees must look inward and acknowledge the facts of any given situation. Everyone in the organization has had a hand in creating what exists. Everyone is responsible for creating the organization and world they want to live in. It's not an option to give that power away or to try to wrest it from others. To abandon caretaking and create an adult culture, each and every individual who comprises the organization must begin to explicitly acknowledge that he or she is responsible for his or her emotional welfare and motivation. And we need to acknowledge that *everyone's* committed participation is needed for the best possible results.

In upcoming chapters, we'll show how new conversations can help make that transformation possible.

Chapter Five

" Hostages to Disappointment "

We were on a courtesy bus provided by a large hotel chain, heading to the airport. Without provocation, the bus driver began haranguing his captive audience about how terrible it was to work for the hotel. The management was unjust, he said, the employees were exploited, the practices and policies were stupid and unfair. On the fifteen-minute ride to the airport, everyone was held hostage as his critical rant persisted. Upon arrival at the airport, we were all experts about the failures of this hotel in its treatment of employees and customers. Relieved to get off, we boarded our flight hoping the same kind of monologue wasn't on the pilot's agenda.

After that incident, we asked ourselves, "How is it that a large organization like that hotel chain has employees who will represent it to customers in such negative and deprecating terms? How does a business survive this?"

Employee cynicism is not restricted to the hotel business. Listen to the conversations you have at work. Listen to the conversations employees have among themselves at any place of business. When you're at the grocery store, the mall, restaurants, the airport, or the bank, pay attention to how people are conversing about their jobs. We've even heard call-center service representatives trashing their employers as their customers listen helplessly on the other end of the line. Disappointed employees spewing their cynicism about the workplace—within earshot of their customers! When that kind of cynicism is so pervasive, what does it say about organizational culture and the conversations that sustain it?

The cynicism that results from disappointment is among the most serious problems faced by organizations today—perhaps even by the world as a whole. Think about it: we have no shortage of knowledge, technology, methods, resourcefulness, creativity, or ingenuity. But when a population sees the world as a disappointing place to be and, as a result, chooses to withhold hope, optimism, and commitment, none of the other qualities can be employed to fullest advantage. Cynicism is without a doubt the largest obstacle to change and progress.

The world *is* a disappointing place, and we all have an overabundance of data to support that view. When we work in organizations, with groups large or small, we always ask people to raise their hands if they've never been disappointed. The response is usually laughter, and often a rueful shaking of the head. Never, so far, have we seen a raised hand.

Changing the conversations related to disappointment is probably the single most significant thing that can be done to change the parent–child culture and improve business results. It's also one of the most difficult changes to effect because it requires constant attention to personal transformation.

In our consulting business, we are often called in to help organizations implement change initiatives or to assist in resolving business problems that have the organization stymied. Sometimes the organization is in crisis. We conduct interviews with a significant number of people in the organization to get a sense of what it is like to work there. Almost always, their comments are a reflection of the many ways they have been disappointed. Although the organizations vary in every conceivable way, employees' reactions and comments are always similar. Most of these reactions can be grouped into three categories:

- **This place is unjust.**

  "We get blamed for the problems they created."

  "They got us into this big mess, and now they want us to work harder with fewer resources to get them out of it."

  "If they had taken our suggestions more seriously and supported us, we wouldn't be in this situation."

  "All they care about are profit margins and squeezing more work out of us."

  "I'm on salary and get paid the same if I work forty hours or fifty, while they can rack up the overtime."

  "I have to punch a time clock and worry about being a few minutes late back from lunch, and they can come and go as they please."

- **This place doesn't take me seriously.**

  "We are the ones doing this work—you'd think they would want our input on how to fix the problems."

  "I have given them suggestions for improving things, but there is never any follow-through."

"They don't want to hear what I have to say. They just want us to keep our mouths shut and work."

- **This place treats me as invisible.**

"I can't make a difference here. I don't have any power. I'm just a cog in the machine."

"It doesn't matter what we do, nothing changes. I've given up."

"I do my job, but a lot of people aren't doing their jobs, and more people are like them than like me."

"We have no voice around here. I have made suggestions and they don't care."

Kind of makes you want to stay in bed, doesn't it? And staying in bed is one of the business results of a failure to deal effectively with disappointment. High absenteeism, low morale, lower quality, cost overruns, and other unacceptable business results are common symptoms in organizations that haven't found a way to effectively deal with cynicism.

A cynic is defined as "a person who distrusts other people and believes that everything is done for selfish reasons" and "a person who has little faith in the integrity or sincerity of others." When a significant number of people in the work population choose to respond to disappointment by distrusting others and viewing others' actions as selfish, they are *choosing* cynicism. The opposite of cynicism is optimism, an expression of hope for the future. How can cynical conversations be good for business when, in order to survive, the focus must be on creating a better future?

Cynical conversations create vicious, self-perpetuating cycles that rely on a disappointing view of history to predict the future. Because we have plenty of data to show why things haven't worked in the past, we convince ourselves—and try to convince others—that things won't work in the future. Cynicism is easily disguised as realism and those who don't share it are cast as naïve. Cynics pour their energies into looking for hidden motives and signs of exploitation to bolster their arguments that change won't work. With a cynic, you can't even expect an open mind, much less hope and commitment. The best you will get is compliance or the appearance of compliance. At the first sign of difficulty, the first hint of disappointment, they will have fresh data to support their arguments: "See? I told you this wouldn't work. This place will never change."

In cynicism, we can find a sense of solidarity and belonging in a community of others who have been disappointed. Cynicism also makes us feel superior and self-righteous when things fail: "If they had only asked [or if they had only listened], I could have told them this ridiculous idea wouldn't work." And finally, in choosing cynicism, we let ourselves off the hook for finding or implementing solutions. If we are not optimistic about creating a better future here, why should we commit ourselves to making contributions outside our job descriptions?

Although it would be easy to say you can stop cynicism if you can stop disappointment, how is that possible? We have an acquaintance who says, "If you don't want to be disappointed, don't have any expectations!" While this may be true (even though it too is cynical), we have yet to find a way to do this. In his writings, even the Dalai Lama has talked about continuously wrestling with disappointment.

Cynical conversations are so bad for business that successfully changing this one dynamic could have a bigger impact on organizational culture and improving business results than almost anything else. Cynicism is the single most inhibiting factor to our ability to sustain change, and our conversations continuously reinforce this inhibition. In addition, vast amounts of time and energy are spent trying to win over cynics, which is a futile endeavor because the data is, and will always be, on their side. The cynic argues concrete history and the optimist offers a prediction of the future that requires suspension of disbelief. There is no risk in staking your claim to the past. It feels enormously risky, even naïve, to have hope in the face of an established history of disappointment.

Typically, cynics at work are dealt with in two ways, and both hurt the organization. One way is trying to convince the cynic that "this time it will be different." You resort to bargaining with them or making promises about the future to enlist their commitment. It's a cheerleading conversation: "Yes, I know we've had a losing season so far, but now we have a new coach and uniforms! Our fans will cheer us on! If you'll just be a team player, this time we'll win for sure! Rah! Rah! Rah!"

The second way colludes with the cynic. Not only do you agree with their cynicism, you pour a little gasoline onto the fire: "Yeah, it is awful! This is a terrible place to be. Nothing ever changes. These people are idiots. It's probably just going to get worse."

In his book *The Answer to How Is Yes*, Peter Block addresses another derivative of this cynical conversation. It centers on asking and answering the question "How?" over and over with no satisfaction. Block writes, "When no answer satisfies, and people continue to act as if they do not understand, then the wrong question is being asked. Then the question about 'How?' is not for information, but is a defense against an alternative and unpredictable future."

Diffusing these kinds of conversations is the most essential step for creating a new culture, and not surprisingly, it's the most difficult. No leader, no matter how talented, can eradicate cynicism with techniques such as inspirational speeches or revised policies and procedures. Cynicism can only be removed one individual at a time—hence we must all start with the person in the mirror. This change requires an awareness of how *you* respond to disappointing circumstances. The cynical cycle can only be broken by personal transformation, by an individual's ongoing commitment to deal with disappointment in a different way.

We know of one worker who did this while working in a call center for a fast-growing, high-tech company. Among other things, this company sells website domains and provides tools and support for building websites. Day after day on the phones, Sean found himself having conversations with frustrated customers who were calling for the second, third, or fourth time because other call-center employees hadn't adequately helped them. He started resenting that he had to clean up other people's messes. He wondered why workers weren't given better training, or why they weren't more committed to helping customers solve problems correctly the first time. He went to his supervisor and suggested that the company provide better training. His supervisor told him to stop worrying about how other people were doing their jobs and to focus on how he handled his own calls. It wasn't Sean's job to worry about training, the supervisor told him, "Just go back to the phones."

Sean was understandably disappointed. He had pointed out a problem, suggested a solution, and his employer had not taken him seriously. "They don't want to hear what I have to say. They don't care about improving the business. They just want us to keep our mouths shut and work." Sean had all the data he needed to choose cynicism based on his disappointment. If he had, that would be the end of this story. Instead, he chose a path of hope and commitment. He wanted to stay engaged, but he didn't know what to do. We helped him craft a plan that would facilitate him living out his commitment.

First, Sean began keeping a chart. When he talked to customers, he wrote down how many of them were calling for the second, third, or fourth time. Then he asked customers how much time they had spent with other customer support employees on previous phone calls. He charted how much more time he had to spend on calls with people who had previously been given bad advice. After a month or so, he wrote a report outlining what it was costing the business when call-center employees didn't have the knowledge, expertise, or commitment to help customers on the first call. His report included how much money was being spent on repeatedly answering the same questions, how much time he (and presumably others) would have had to field new calls if he hadn't been cleaning up unresolved issues. His report also contained customers' feedback about the frustration they had with the call center and the way it affected their views of the company.

Within a few weeks, the company created a position of training manager, with the assigned role of creating learning and coaching programs to improve customer service and reduce costs by training employees to give higher quality responses in less time. They asked Sean if he would take the job, and he did. Over the next year, the number of repeat calls dropped significantly, saving the company money and significantly improving customer satisfaction. Sean was promoted again several months later to become a product development manager in charge of new product launches.

After Sean had been working in his new job for a significant amount of time, we asked him to think about his situation and to complete these four statements, an exercise we frequently use as part of our work with clients:

- I feel helpless when _____ .
- I lose hope and optimism when _____ .
- I withhold my commitment when _____ .
- The promise I want from others to restore the above is

_____ .

His answers, as do most people's, centered on what others had done to him to make him feel helpless, to lose hope, and to withhold his commitment. When he talked about the promise he wanted from others to restore his commitment and willingness to act—to take him seriously, be respectful about his suggestions, include him in decision making, and so on—Sean had an epiphany. He realized that his optimism, hope, commitment, and empowerment were all connected to *someone else doing or providing something to him.* He was giving away his power by tying his choice for hope and optimism to someone else's behavior. This sets up a condition that guarantees continued cynicism. When you tie your choices for hope and optimism to someone else, it is just a matter of time before you're disappointed again and add to your treasure trove of data to harden your cynical outlook.

The business ramifications of a culture characterized by disappointment and cynicism are enormous. Changing that one dynamic costs no money, but it is one of the most daunting changes for an organization to undertake. It requires us to grow up and put aside our childish responses to disappointment. It means committing to hope and optimism in the face of the cynicism of others. It requires that we recognize the choice inherent in our response to disappointing circumstances. It means we have to find a way to sincerely say "thank you" when people tell us we are naïve, foolish, and unrealistic for choosing optimism.

Changing the conversations about disappointment, accountability, caretaking, and commitment is the only way to create true and lasting change. We'll use the next chapters to look at how to do this by making new personal commitments, choosing authentic conversations, using different language, and framing issues in a new way.

Chapter Six

" Change the Conversation, Change the Culture "

W hat will workplace conversations sound like if people are no longer talking to each other in the ways they used to? When compliance is no longer the organizing principle, how does that change the way they engage each other?

Until now, we have been focusing on conversations that support traditional relationships and parent–child cultures. We have made a case for the business and relationship problems these cause and how they profoundly inhibit change, marketplace response, and business results. We have dealt briefly with the possibility of new conversations and what they might include. The purpose of this chapter is to delve beyond these initial looks. We construct the fundamental nature of the changes required for sustaining adult relationships and creating a new culture. We also present a general framework for new conversations.

Confronting the initial change in workplace conversations and sustaining that change for the long term are extremely challenging and can feel daunting. Underneath the conversations themselves are significant emotional issues that each of us must deal with. You have to be willing to articulate your doubt about yourself, even if you fear the vulnerability this creates. You have to summon the courage to raise difficult issues in a culture where that is seen as being a "whiner," someone who is uncooperative or even a troublemaker. It requires reframing your thinking to consider your contribution to the good of the whole, when you have been accustomed to plotting how to get ahead and make your own department look good. You have to confront within yourself what it means to be committed, to be accountable, and to take responsibility for your contribution to a problem or difficult situation. You have to be willing to let go of old disappointments and forgive others—and yourself. You must no longer view your job as a way to make a living, but as an opportunity to create your own future, engage others with a shared purpose, and infuse your life with meaning.

Reflecting on what you have to give up to do these things is an important step. You must be able to deal with your losses if you expect to benefit from the gains. If you're not willing to lose the ability to blame someone else when things start looking shaky, you won't get the benefit of knowing the future is yours to create. If you cling to the comfort of doing things the way you always have, you won't experience the excitement and satisfaction of relationships built on honesty and trust. This kind of change is intensely personal. It is impossible to overemphasize the importance of personal transformation in creating authentic conversations.

For true cultural change to happen, new conversations must remain at the adult–adult level. We all grew up in environments riddled with parent–child conversations. These patterns of engagement are what we have relied on for most of our lives. Even with daily, conscious effort, engaging in parent–child relationships and the associated conversations can be an extraordinarily tough habit to break.

Although traditional conversations and relationships are damaging to a business, one of their virtues is that they are predictable. They feel familiar. We know how to respond to each other in those conversations—just like in a family, where the children know their roles and the parents know theirs. Each has developed finely honed responses. Around the kitchen table, conversational stimuli are fully expected and predictable, as are the responses and the emotions to which they are connected.

One of the first things to acknowledge when changing workplace conversations is that the world of consistency goes away. Engaging in this new way puts relationships at risk in an environment where relationships feel paramount. We each have a history of behavior upon which our relationships are based. Maybe you say "can do" even when you have serious doubts about whether it can be done. Maybe you feel you must always appear in control because of perceived cultural rewards. Maybe you choose silence instead of making constructive suggestions because you fear looking foolish. This behavior history is challenged when you alter the way you engage others. It doesn't feel familiar anymore and may even feel frightening.

You can prepare yourself by becoming a better listener, managing your emotional responses in the moment, and acknowledging that your perspective is only one of many legitimate views. The old, rote responses no longer serve, and feelings that you typically submerge must be confronted and expressed. In new workplace conversations, we face each other without expectation, without defense, without a directive, without a predictable response in the moment. If you choose not to play the role of the parent or the child, who are you? Who am I?

Each new conversation means creating moments where you are unsure. It requires great courage.

What Do Adult–Adult Relationships Look Like?

To create and sustain adult relationships, people must make a number of critical agreements. We frame these agreements as a set of rights and responsibilities. These are the rights we claim and the responsibilities we choose. Claiming rights without responsibilities is anarchy. Responsibilities without rights is oppression. Consenting to rights *and* responsibilities is necessary for us to claim our place as adults.

The rights and responsibilities we propose look like this:

Each individual becomes the eyes and the voice of the business.

This means it is no longer all right to isolate yourself or let others isolate themselves. You can no longer afford to remain blind to the fortunes of the whole enterprise or ignore the difficult issues that must be raised and resolved. To be the voice of the business means to develop an *informed* viewpoint about what's going on in the business, the difficult issues, and the prospects for the future. It means putting the success of the whole before personal ambition.

Each individual brings an independent point of view and is open to others' perspectives.

Though you are committed to being the voice of the business, you realize your voice is one of many. We all make sense of the same data in different ways. Each person will bring an independent point of view about defining the issues, what changes are needed, and where attention should be focused. You expect and embrace passionate, heated discussions and dissent. You do not back away from conflicts, because when people bring their points of view and care deeply about them, conflict is inevitable. Together we find a way to manage conflict so that resolution is neither victory nor defeat.

While valuing dissent, it is mitigated when you make yourself open to the influence of others. Leadership is no longer defined as "having the right answers," but as an ability to engage others to find the best solutions. By doing this, you avoid the pitfall of having to be right, insisting on your own way, or having to win. You cultivate the ability to reframe how you see things based on how others see them. Together we search for solutions that take everyone's viewpoints into account—as long as they serve the business. This is the heart of collaboration.

As Margaret J. Wheatley writes in *Leadership and the New Science*,

> We need a constantly expanding array of data, views, and interpretations if we are to make wise sense of the world. We need to include more and more eyes. We need to be constantly asking: "Who else should be here? Who else should be looking at this?" . . . An organization rich with many interpretations develops a wiser sense of what is going on and what needs to be done. Such organizations become more intelligent.

Each individual is expected to raise difficult issues.

In adult relationships, people are expected to raise difficult issues directly, simply, and explicitly, without aggression or hostility. Previously in the work environment, you could feel safe in ignoring these issues because they were someone else's responsibility. Now you raise and confront difficult issues because doing so makes a difference to your work relationships and to the business. You make it clear by engaging and confronting these issues that you are committed and passionate about success. When raising difficulties, you avoid blame and criticism, give others the benefit of the doubt, forsake cynicism, own your contributions, and focus on resolution.

Each individual extends a spirit of goodwill to the endeavor.

No matter how tough the issues and difficult the realities, you choose to bring goodwill to business conversations and manage your own emotional responses. Goodwill is not a feeling. It is a conscious choice you make about how you will engage with other people. Extending goodwill means viewing others not as adversaries, but as business partners to whom you are committed. At the same time, goodwill means you tell the truth as you see it. Your words and intentions are spoken out of commitment to the business and to your coworkers. You are responsible for bringing your goodwill into the room, and do not use it to barter or negotiate. You do not predicate your goodwill on the beliefs or behaviors of others.

Each individual creates business literacy in others.

You choose to increase and spread business literacy. You expect to fully inform those around you of everything you know that is relevant to the business. You expect to create literacy with others about your understanding of the business, and expect them to do the same for you. Barring extenuating circumstances, there are no secrets regarding information pertinent to the business. What you know should be okay for everyone else to know. Information must be open to anyone. It is your responsibility to initiate opportunities to distribute knowledge by teaching and openness to learning. Unless we are all fully informed, we cannot be partners. Joining together to distribute business literacy becomes everyone's responsibility.

Each individual chooses accountability for the success of the whole business.

This commitment recognizes that the business is a collection of interdependent units and relationships. Maximizing one at the expense of others is detrimental to the success of the whole. Sometimes a unit, product, or process may require specific attention, and people might be inclined to feel resentful about dealing with the ramifications. Choosing accountability for the whole helps you take these situations into account without resentment because you understand the business reasons behind the decisions and give them your support. You recognize that we are all in this together and that *our* success is more important than yours or mine or any single department's. This also speaks to the heart of collaboration.

Think about the way traditional organizations manage their budgets. When you prepare a budget forecast for the upcoming year, what's the routine? You ask for more than you want so that when the budget is inevitably cut, you will have what you need. What happens if there is a surplus in the fourth quarter? Hurry, find a way to spend it or we'll lose it next year! What if another department could use that money to finish an important project? Too bad for them. They can't have *our* money. How might the budgeting process and conversations change if everyone took accountability for the whole?

Each individual manages his or her own morale, motivation, and commitment.

Although you support others, you do not take responsibility for their emotional welfare or expect others to do this for you. You resist the impulse to blame others when things go wrong and instead look for understanding and resolution of the issues. You discover what your contribution to the problem has been and make it public *before* you take it on yourself to articulate how others contributed to the problem. One of the most powerful adult positions you can take is showing goodwill and commitment by saying, "As I reflect on this issue, I want to acknowledge what I have done. Here is how I have contributed to this difficult situation." You choose to hold yourself accountable for the part you played in creating the problem, rather than waiting for someone to catch you. You stop expecting others to motivate you and take responsibility for your own morale.

A Final Word About Adult Relationships

Disappointment is inevitable. In adult relationships, we *will* disappoint each other.

Even with good intentions, there will be times when we don't fully inform each other and times when we won't muster goodwill. Sometimes we will withhold rather than share relevant information, obscure rather than raise the difficult issues. We may fall into silence rather than expressing our viewpoint.

Here's an example from our own life—two people who have been working on authentic conversations for years. Early one afternoon, Maren suggested going to a local music club that night, and Jamie agreed. After several hours of running errands, however, going to the club to dance and hear music seemed less appealing to Jamie.

"How important is it to you that we go out tonight?" Jamie asked Maren. She got a look of disappointment and her mood changed almost instantly. "Well, if you don't want to go, then it's fine. We won't go."

Jamie broke the tense silence in the car on the way home: "You seem disappointed. I really hate disappointing you." Maren remained mute and simmering.

We spent two heated hours untangling the knot that resulted from that inauthentic conversation—and we reluctantly admit that there was a shortage of goodwill. After we were finally able to debrief the argument calmly, the following points emerged:

- Jamie didn't want to go out, but instead of stating it directly, he asked Maren how important it was to her to go.

- Maren had been looking forward to going out and was disappointed by Jamie's question. Instead of saying that directly, she said, "Fine. We won't go." And then she pouted.

- Jamie realized that it wasn't disappointing Maren that he hated, it was dealing with her reaction to that disappointment.

- Maren realized it didn't serve the relationship to say one thing when she clearly felt another.

We did not go out to the club that night, but we did learn some valuable lessons about being authentic and about forgiveness. What is important in such moments of disappointment is the choice you make in response. It is easy to lapse into blame and recrimination: "Well, you haven't kept your commitments. We were supposed to have this different kind of relationship, and you blew it." When you experience those all-too-familiar child-like feelings of disappointment, the temptation is to fall back on the familiar ways of responding to it. No matter how many languages you learn, when the hammer hits your thumb, you swear in your native tongue. If you consistently revert to old ways of seeing situations and the traditional, more comfortable ways of behaving, true change is at risk. If you decide the failures of others give you an excuse for letting yourself off the hook, new conversations will wither on the vine. The roots of a parent–child culture will burrow even deeper.

You can make a different choice. You can choose engagement and goodwill. If you are going to be an adult, you cannot use your disappointment in others as an excuse to divorce yourself from your own commitments. If you self-destruct during a moment of disappointment, you are saying that your commitment is contingent on others. But true commitment is doing what you believe is right, regardless of what happens. True commitment asks you to see disappointment, breakdowns, and pain as opportunities for personal growth.

Even more difficult is dealing with a situation in which you disappoint yourself. It is enormously tempting to fall into helplessness and despair and to give up. The healthy choice in the face of self-disappointment is to say, "Okay, a moment of failure." Like a baby who is learning to walk, pick yourself up and get ready to try again. Renew the commitment and resolve to make a different choice the next time.

Four Common Elements in the New Conversation

Once we embrace the commitments, we acknowledge each other as adults and begin new conversations. But you don't have to wait for the whole organization to get on board to make the change. You can change the culture in the moment, in any room. What does that sound like?

Remember our friend Joe, the newspaper publisher we discussed in the introduction? When he spoke at the large group meeting, four critical elements were part of the conversation.

Honestly acknowledge the difficult issues and name the harsh reality.

Adults must acknowledge reality in order to deal with unpredictability, anxiety, frustration, and cynicism. They state the facts as they understand them and realize that others have different and valid points of view. To deny this is to deny our collective experience. Joe told the newspaper's employees, "The newspaper is in deep trouble, and I don't have all the answers. I need your help to find solutions." He gave them the big picture, acknowledged the difficult issues, and invited others to embrace the difficulty and work together to resolve the issues.

State your contribution to the difficult issues and acknowledge its harmful effects.

By owning your contributions, you take responsibility for your actions and invite others to examine their own contributions to the difficulty. We often get asked, "What if I haven't contributed to the difficult issue?" Contributions can be acts of commission (something you did) or they can be acts of omission (something you ignored or didn't do). Acts of omission are also contributions, and anyone involved in an enterprise has contributed in one way or another. Joe admitted his contribution was "trying to make all of you feel better, safer, and more secure." Employees could consider that their contribution was not making themselves literate about the business or choosing to blame others without examining and acknowledging how they failed to contribute to the success of the whole.

The adult response, which is often difficult to muster, is to examine and own your contribution. Stating it out loud is a daring act of personal accountability. What we acknowledge allows us to honestly examine the world together.

State the risks and acknowledge difficulties, including the possibility that things might not work out.

The truth is you can never know the future. To pretend you can is both dishonest and demeaning to others. It doesn't serve anyone to soften the truth or to insist on putting a positive spin on an uncertain future. Denial is dangerous. Joe frankly admitted, "Right now, I don't know how we are going to solve these difficult problems." By admitting this, Joe was inviting the employees to become involved. When the future is uncertain and risks are explicit, we see how vital it is to work together for a solution.

Frame choices about how you can engage the future.

Ultimately, you will be accountable for the choices you make. Even a decision not to change or to do nothing is a choice that comes with natural consequences. You choose whether you will authentically try to make something succeed or surrender to your sense of failure.

A number of choices will be faced in this fourth step, but the relationship choice is primary. To have any hope for success, we must all choose to take responsibility for collaborating with each other and for managing our own disappointment. We must move closer, we must engage. As adults, we choose to increase our ability to cope with potential failure rather than retreating into the childish hope that somebody else will take care of it for us. Joe said, "You are going to have to account for your own future here and the future of the paper. We all have choices to make going forward. I hope you will do everything you can to help solve these problems."

A Word About Personal Transformation

To make new conversations authentic and transforming, clarity about your own intention is essential. This requires self-awareness and a willingness to be honest and vulnerable. You reveal your uncertainty instead of trying to appear as though you have it together and under control. If you manage people at work, this is probably antithetical to just about everything you have learned about managing and motivating others. But it is the path to building an adult culture.

Personal transformation comes first. It is the most important work. If you can't choose hope and optimism, you can't expect that of others. If you can't face the harsh reality of difficult issues, you can't raise them with others. If you are not willing to state your purpose publicly and ask others to hold you accountable, you can't expect others to choose to be accountable. You cannot help others create what you cannot create for yourself.

Chapter Seven

" Moving from Manipulation to Engagement "

One staple of our workshops is a list of conversation techniques that are often used for manipulation and effect. We created this list off the top of our heads, and it was dishearteningly easy to make. We simply named techniques we commonly used or experienced others using.

Language used for effect means choosing words and a message aimed at creating an effect in another. It is the language we choose when we're trying to elicit a specific reaction. It's the language people choose when they want to make others feel guilty, to shame them, calm them down, flatter them, or even to motivate them. It might sound like "You're not going to eat this after all the trouble I went to prepare it?" or "Maybe you'd get more accomplished if you weren't spending so much time gossiping in the break room," or "Why are you getting so angry? You're blowing things all out of proportion."

Language for manipulation is a method for getting what you want without being direct about it or without giving the person you are talking to the benefit of a bigger picture. If you're direct about trying to win another person over to your side, for instance, that is not manipulation. But if you intend to get someone to do something or to see things in a certain way without disclosing your intention, that is manipulation.

It is an interesting human phenomenon. Most people say they know when they are being manipulated, and they probably do. Yet we all think we're so sharp that others won't get it when we are trying to manipulate them. In fact, most people are so accustomed to operating this way that they don't even realize they are being manipulative.

Here's a story to illustrate what we mean. We have a young grandson whose company we enjoy immensely. From time to time, our son would call us to inquire about babysitting services, although he didn't usually ask directly. He would say something like "Hey, Mom, how would you like to spend some quality time with your favorite grandson?"

One day, Maren's response was "Honey, I appreciate that you need a babysitter, and we're always happy to help out if we can. But could you just ask me directly instead of using all this language for manipulation? You know, that's something we talk about a lot in our workshops."

"Really? You teach that?" he said, his voice charged with excitement. "I want to learn how to manipulate people!"

It's a funny story, even though it made us shake our heads. That point of view—teach me how to manipulate better—is so acceptable in our society and work cultures that we see it as a desirable skill: "Manipulate the message to get what you want." The media does it, politicians do it, parents do it, husbands and wives do it, kids do it, and our most visible corporate leaders do it. Just try to get through the day without a good manipulation or two.

To further examine language for manipulation, let's deconstruct the babysitting story. Our son needed a babysitter. His *intention* in the conversation was to manipulate Mom to get what he wanted, and so he chose *techniques* to support that intention. The conversation he created was inauthentic.

It is essential to understand the connection between your intentions and the techniques you employ to live them out if you truly want to change your conversations. It's the only way to create a culture based on honesty, commitment, and collaboration.

Intention answers the question "What?" What do I want to be in the world? What is my purpose? What do I want to create? What do I want to do?

Techniques are what you use to carry out your intentions. They answer the question "How?" Techniques are the tools, processes, methods, tactics, and activities that support your intentions. Most of us spend vast amounts of time and energy obsessing about the "How?" without giving sufficient attention to the "What?" Clarifying your intentions before you choose techniques will result in more authenticity.

To help illustrate this relationship, consider the scalpel, a tool commonly used by surgeons. Dr. Christiaan Barnard, who pioneered open-heart surgery in the 1960s, used the scalpel to save thousands of lives. The same tool in the hands of Jack the Ripper was used to cut women up in little pieces. Exact same tool— different intentions.

In conversations, the major difference between language for manipulation and effect and language for disclosure and engagement lies in your intention. Words are tools. How you use them are techniques. Your intentions drive whether the conversation becomes manipulative.

If you want to have authentic conversations, it is essential to be clear about your intentions. In the babysitting example, the intention was to manipulate Mom into babysitting. Our son chose language designed to appeal to Mom's underlying emotions—desire to spend time with her favorite (and only) grandson or guilt about not spending enough time with her grandson. But quality time with her grandson wasn't the issue, and they both knew it. Our son was in a jam and needed a babysitter. In an effort to get what he wanted, he disguised his agenda. (Guess where he learned some of the finer points of those techniques?)

This example may be obvious, but in many cases, the ways we use language for manipulation are so nuanced and so much a part of our culture, they are nearly invisible. Scratch the surface of much of the leadership training and "motivational" material available in the marketplace, and you'll discover that the heart of it consists of helping people learn how to be better manipulators. Models, formulas, and scripts are designed to help people use language for manipulation more effectively. Training or advice that tells you to speak to someone else's self-interest means heading down the path of manipulation. If your intention is to motivate others, even if the cause is worthy, manipulation is certainly in play.

Management by Manipulation

What makes manipulation so compelling? Why are our conversations so riddled with manipulative language?

Manipulation is compelling because we have all learned it is an effective way to get what we want. It makes it easier to win in the moment. You can use it to make yourself look better and maybe even get people to like you. Manipulation can get results. It can get you the promotion. It can get you elected. Without question, it can be a powerful means to your end result. But it is costly. Manipulation creates a barrier to authentic conversation. In the long run, it takes a toll on relationships by destroying trust and fostering cynicism. You are creating something you can't really believe in.

Some time ago, we worked with a manager who supervised the copy desk at a major metropolitan newspaper in the Southeast. The copy desk is the last stop before ink hits paper. Copy editors must be creative. They must be meticulous about detail and accuracy under constant deadline pressure. Their work is demanding, stressful, and underappreciated. At this paper, high employee turnover and a series of high-profile news events that required extra coverage meant that copy editors and page designers were being asked to work a lot of overtime. The way in which they were asked, however, became a source of resentment.

The manager would approach a staffer at his or her desk and say, "Good news! I have an overtime opportunity for you." For someone who had already worked twelve days straight and was longing for a day off, it was neither good news nor an opportunity. They both knew it, and the people who overheard the conversations knew it. Although the paper was confronting a difficult business issue, copy editors and page designers began coming in to work prepared with reasons why they couldn't work overtime, just in case. They avoided answering their phones when they had a day off. When the manager wasn't around, staffers began to call out to each other sarcastically, "Hey, buddy, I have a headline opportunity for you." The reply would often be something like "Oh yeah? Well, I have an intern's grammar and accuracy opportunity for you."

Copy editors weren't being kept apprised of management efforts to fix the staff shortage, nor were they enlisted for their help to come up with creative solutions that could have eased overtime or difficult scheduling issues. They resented being pressured to work overtime in such a disingenuous way. People began updating their résumés and looking for ways to get out, exacerbating the turnover problem.

This manager wasn't a bad person and probably didn't see herself as being manipulative. She often got what she wanted in the short term. But because she used language for manipulation rather than being direct about needing help to resolve a difficult business issue, the employees felt lied to, disrespected, and resentful.

Making a List, Checking It Twice

The following list outlines some of the conversational techniques used for manipulation and effect. This list is by no means complete. Note how many you see used in the workplace, and pay particular attention to your personal favorites.

- Appealing to an underlying emotion (guilt, desire, etc.)
- Creating fictions, lying
- Denying or avoiding difficult truths
- Disguising agendas
- Exaggerating optimism or pessimism
- Feigning interest
- Giving inauthentic praise
- Name dropping
- Offering cosmetic support or safety
- Overpromising
- Overstating threats, opportunities, or urgency
- Providing a partial picture of reality
- Providing calculated descriptions

- Using humor inappropriately to deflect or distract

- Using sarcasm

- Withholding relevant information

This is our list, and we might have missed a few of your favorites. Take a few moments to reflect on which ones you have used and which have been used on you. Because manipulation is so common, people don't always realize they're using these techniques out of self-interest. One workshop participant, shaking his head in confusion, asked us, "So if I tell someone I think they really look nice today, that's manipulation?" We replied, "What do you think?" His brow furrowed and he was silent for a few moments. He finally said, "Well, I guess it would depend if I was telling them that so they would like me or so they would do something for me." It was a moment of clarity that intention is at the heart of manipulation, not technique.

It is not easy to give up these time-tested, tried-and-true techniques. You may see them as effective or as essential for your survival at work. When given the opportunity to understand why these techniques are so compelling, people routinely express anxiety and apprehension about the risks associated with giving them up. They ask, "Without using manipulation, how will I ever get what I want?"

Conversations are our primary method for creating and sustaining change. How is transformation to an adult culture possible if we continue using manipulative conversational tactics? True change requires us to examine our intentions and to choose new techniques (language and conversations) to support those intentions.

Remember our newspaper executive Joe and his message about the difficult issues the paper faced in the marketplace? With coaching and enormous personal courage, he took a stand.

He changed his conversational intentions and, in the moment, abandoned language for manipulation and effect. He turned away from his customary tactics of exaggerating optimism and overpromising. He acknowledged his role in helping employees avoid difficult truths surrounding the serious problems that were threatening the newspaper's survival. He directly told employees what he wanted: their ingenuity and commitment to find solutions to problems in partnership.

When he finally told the truth, he got a standing ovation. He had treated people like the adults they were. When he asked for their help and support in finding solutions to problems, he took a difficult and essential first step in changing the parent–child culture. He invited the adults he worked with to show up and participate in resolving difficult business issues.

In Joe's new conversation with the employees, he used techniques from another list, which we call "Using Language for Disclosure and Engagement":

- Acknowledging doubt and failure

- Acknowledging your own contribution to problems

- Choosing authentic conversations

- Directly naming the difficult issues

- Disclosing

- Extending goodwill

- Framing choices

- Making a commitment to an action or result

- Taking the other side

- Telling the truth

In our workshops, most people tell us they would prefer to have others talk to them in these ways. They say these techniques are useful for engaging other people authentically. They also tell us that they already use some of these techniques. Then they quickly begin citing the possible negative consequences of disclosing and engaging authentically in the workplace, with comments like these:

> "Subordinates can't have that kind of relationship with management."
>
> "What if people don't like me? What if they get angry?"
>
> "I can't tell the truth to my boss."
>
> "People don't really want to hear the truth."
>
> "If I admit to my employees I'm partially to blame for the situation, how can I supervise them effectively?"
>
> "People don't really need to see the big picture to do their job."
>
> "Sometimes it is better if people do it my way."
>
> "If I tell the truth, I might not get what I want."
>
> "Using these techniques would create too much tension."
>
> "Language for effect takes the edge off."
>
> "If I started using language for disclosure and engagement, it would put all my relationships at risk. It's not safe—I'd get fired!"

It's clear from these comments that we have created a business culture so invested in winning and staying safe that telling the truth seems perilous. Confronting the choice for authentic conversations creates a sort of paralysis: "I know it's the right thing to do but it feels too risky. I'd make myself too vulnerable."

We've pointed out the risks of using language for manipulation and effect. The inherent risks in using language for disclosure and engagement are also real and provoke anxiety. These risks come with consequences. When people think about making the commitment for new conversational techniques, they do a risk/consequence assessment: which set of risks and consequences do I prefer?

A good friend of ours who works as a therapist told us that making a choice doesn't eliminate problems. You only determine which set of problems you want to deal with. If you choose language for engagement and commit to telling the truth, then you have to be accountable for your beliefs and point of view. On the other hand, if you choose language for manipulation, by feigning interest in someone to get something from him or her, you risk being seen as phony and you build a relationship on something you don't believe in. You might not be more likely to buy a car from a salesman who told you, "I really need to make this sale today because my mortgage payment is due." But you'd probably respect his honesty and direct approach.

Clarifying Your Intentions

In the end, choosing authentic conversations means getting clear about intentions. To achieve that clarity, ask yourself: Who do I want to be? What is it I want to stand for when no one is looking? What do I believe in, and what do I want to create in my life? These are all high-stakes questions.

It's no accident that manipulative conversations create and perpetuate a parent–child culture. To have these conversations, you need to see others as objects, "things" to be used as a means to your end. Such conversations denigrate the experience of others. They ignore the freedom and will of the individual. They reinforce policies, procedures, and practices to ensure compliance and alignment because people are seen as lazy and untrustworthy. When you choose manipulation, you delude yourself into thinking that you aren't accountable for your actions. You look to leadership, experts, and authority to make all the important decisions and to create your world for you. Or you tell yourself that you are the only one who can make things happen, and withhold information, overpromise, or disguise your agenda.

Choosing manipulation as a strategy for "selling" change means insisting that the dominant and relevant reality is based on roles and responsibilities, job descriptions, procedures and policies. It attempts to negate individual accountability. It means selling corporate visions and values, and if people don't buy in, inventing ways to make them comply anyway. When you assume people won't *choose* to be accountable, much of your time and energy is expended on making sure people are *held* accountable.

When our change strategies are based on disclosure and engagement, we create a culture where people are viewed and treated as individuals with freedom, choice, and accountability. *This only acknowledges the reality of individual choice.* Conversations are imbued with full disclosure of projects and plans, which creates commitment and investment in a shared future. Conversations for disclosure presuppose a faith in people's ability to collaborate and to use their intelligence and goodwill to create a world they can believe in. Instead of command and control, choices are framed. Instead of forced compliance, people choose commitment and accountability. Dissent is encouraged and honored. People authentically engage each other in creating a future for the good of the whole rather than relying on a few to create a future for everyone.

Authentic conversations require that we believe differently and talk differently. Commitment to personal transformation is imperative. Using language techniques of disclosure and engagement while clinging to traditional beliefs about people and their roles in the organization will not work. The result is manipulative. And people get it.

A fundamental and inherent freedom is found here. Personal commitments don't require anyone else to change. On your own, you can embrace a new way of viewing the world, be clear about your intentions, and begin to change the conversations.

The following are eight personal commitments we believe are necessary to begin changing the conversation.

Recognizing Others as Free and Accountable

Organizations traditionally have treated freedom as a problem to be managed. Conversations about getting others to "sign up, get on board, and buy in" to changes are a grudging recognition that each of us is free and constantly making choices. Organizations typically have opted for techniques that result in compliance (time clocks, performance evaluations, policies) rather than holding conversations that acknowledge individual freedom, choice, and the fact that our futures are always at risk. When our conversations reflect caretaking, prescription, and barter, we acknowledge reservations about freedom and accountability in others and ourselves.

Adult cultures recognize and embrace the freedom and accountability that individuals possess. These qualities are confronted and celebrated.

Choosing Engagement over Manipulation

By choosing engagement over manipulation, we send a message that we take people seriously. We resist the temptation to see people as objects to be manipulated. Instead, we choose to engage them with language for disclosure. We focus on collaboration and solutions, not on selling or winning.

Using Language for Disclosure over Effect

Language for disclosure is one of the foundations of partnership, collaboration, and true adult cultures. We commit to be open about plans and projects and how they color the events and people we come into contact with. Disclosure requires that we "put it all on the table." When we disguise agendas, use calculated promises, give inauthentic praise, use deception or other manipulative techniques to get our way, community and partnership are unachievable.

Choosing Consent and Commitment over Compliance

We all understand what it means to give the *appearance* of compliance. We have all said yes when we meant no. We allow the appearance of compliance to lull us into believing that manipulation and mandates work. It can be reassuring to think conversational gimmicks and developing new rules make things run more smoothly. None of these techniques work as much as we imagine they do. Each individual still decides how to respond to what is proposed. Individuals decide how to dispose of what is presented to them or forced upon them. It is simply recognizing reality to acknowledge the individual's choice in commitment and honor his or her consent.

Putting the Relationship at Risk

Telling the truth as we see it does not always go well. It can put our relationships at risk. Sometimes changing a relationship means losing it. In parent–child cultures, many would prefer to have "better parents" rather than grow up and commit to personal honesty. They would prefer reassurance and protection to assuming the responsibilities inherent in adult cultures. "Parents" would rather have control than consent. They would prefer that people listen and do what they are told rather than confront issues of autonomy that every individual possesses.

Growing up is a difficult business. To seek engagement is to live with an uncertain future. Relationships are always at risk. Consciously acknowledging this fact is necessary and sometimes difficult work.

Choosing Contribution and Worth over Self-Interest and Cynicism

Pursuing engagement with unselfish optimism is demanding. It is especially difficult to do in the face of disappointment, indifference, and failure. The temptation to surrender to our inner cynic is constant—after all, the world gives each of us more than enough data to justify our cynical conclusions. Choosing contribution over self-interest and cynicism builds collaboration and extends hope.

Embracing Accountability for the Whole

Whose organization is it, anyway? From the viewpoint of engagement, the organization belongs to everyone who is part of it. Approaching change from this perspective means we recognize the reality of personal freedom and embrace partnership in the pursuit of change. Partnership means that each of us is fully responsible for the success of the whole. Partners care as much about the other's success as they do their own. A strategy based on anything less than consent is almost certain to be frustrated by resistance and sabotage.

Willingness to Grieve and Let Go

Affirming and recognizing others as free uncovers the fact that life offers no guarantees. Our efforts may go unappreciated and unrewarded. The risk of failure is always present. We mourn the loss of what could have been or what didn't work out the way we had hoped. Letting go gives us peace of mind and allows us to move on. Both grieving and letting go are essential for progress.

These commitments are not easy to come by in a traditional organization. They are difficult to make, especially in an environment of risk with no certain rewards. Perseverance is a virtue here, as embracing these commitments is not a one-time event. It is a struggle that requires you to recommit—sometimes daily. You hear the voice that argues for the rewards of embracing these commitments because they are right, good, and significant in their contribution. Another voice tells you that committing would be foolish because it is risky and naïve, or that there is nothing in it for you.

How do you begin to resolve these arguments? Do you have the courage to mindfully create the world in which you want to live even while knowing the risks? Once you can find answers to these questions within yourself, your intentions will become clear. Clarity can create the new conversations that foster adult cultures marked by consent, commitment, and true collaboration.

You may discover that it is really not that hard to just say, "Mom, we made plans to go out with friends Saturday night. Would you be available to babysit?"

Chapter Eight

" Stop Courting the Cynic "

Before you can change the conversation, you need to know who is doing the talking. That observation sounds so obvious that it may not seem worthy of examination, but it's critically important.

The truth is that you wake up every day and choose which part of yourself to send out into the world. To change the conversation, you have to be aware of who is showing up. You can send out the part that is longing to do good work in the world. This part wants to contribute to the greater good, make a difference, and leave a legacy. It's a part that infuses your work with commitment and passion as you go about giving something of value to others. This part aspires to be noble, to be of service, and to create worth.

But you may also find yourself paying attention to the part that is always on alert for the next inevitable letdown, because experience tells you that the world is a disappointing place. You see yourself trying to survive and prosper in a place that seems unjust and uncaring, where you are inevitably hurt and disappointed. This part longs for security, for someone to reassure you that everything will be taken care of. You want protection and safety, not constant reminders that things might not work out and that most things are out of your control.

And finally, there's the part of you that wants to assert your dominance as top dog, the center of the world. This part has difficulty recognizing anything but self-interest, and aggressively goes after whatever it needs so you can come out the winner. It's the part that demands to be in control and looks out for number one. It wants to be in charge regardless of who might get stepped on in the process. After all, if you don't look out for yourself, who will?

Examining Stances

In your waking moments every day, you are considering these different aspects of your makeup. Who do you want to be? Which part of you will ultimately determine how you see things and how you react to them? The ways you choose to experience the world are called *stances*. We have long used these concepts in our workshops, and Peter Block also writes about them extensively in his book *Stewardship: Choosing Service over Self-Interest*. For the sake of simplicity, we'll call the stances we have described service, disappointment, and self-interest. The outcomes of the disappointment and self-interest stances are typically expressed through the voices of a cynic, a victim, or a bystander. They all have a huge influence on conversations.

Cynics withhold hope, optimism, and commitment and yet demand that those with authority never disappoint them. They are, to use the phrase coined by Spiro Agnew, "nattering nabobs of negativism."

Victims refuse to take personal responsibility, but require that those in authority take full responsibility. They are the voices of the powerless. They say things like, "We can't change if they don't change."

And the bystanders are the perennial fence-sitters. They say they have an open mind, but will promise commitment only if someone can *prove* to them that things will work out. They are the voices of "wait and see."

Think about your organization. Do any of these stances sound familiar? How many of your coworkers could be described as having these stances? Do any of the stances sound like you? What kind of effect do they have on conversations at work?

In our workshops, inevitably someone raises a hand and says, "You know, I usually start out my day with optimism and hope, but then I come to work. My boss yells at me, or my coworkers start griping about some policy they think is stupid, or people start bickering about whose turn it is to clean the coffeemaker. The next thing I know, I'm feeling just as cynical and angry as everyone else."

Our response is "Why is that?" Workshop participants get busy explaining why they have no choice but to be infected by others' negative attitudes. It is too hard to make a choice for optimism and faith, they say earnestly, while listening to a constant chorus singing that song with the catchy rhythm and snappy lyrics, "Poor, poor, pitiful me, I am as disappointed as I can be."

Yes, we absolutely agree. It is hard. Very hard. But *why* is it so hard? What is so powerful about this chorus that we feel compelled to jump in with our backup vocals instead of changing the station?

What people begin to see is that jumping in with backup vocals comes naturally because everyone knows the song so well. Don't make the mistake of seeing the cynic, victim, and bystander as "them." The cynic, victim, and bystander live in every single one of us. You, your neighbors, your coworkers—we all help write the music, lyrics, and harmony that make the "Cynic, Victim, Bystander Anthem" sound so familiar. It makes perfect sense that we would know these stances by heart because, let's face it, who hasn't found disappointment in the world? Who among us hasn't felt powerless to make a change in our circumstances? Who hasn't felt the urge to retreat until we know what will be the safest course of action? Who hasn't felt dependent on someone else to create a successful future?

These stances are powerful because they are always alive and well within you. When someone else starts talking about how terrible things are, of course it is easy to get hooked. That is your experience, too! You have plenty of data to confirm that the world is a disappointing place, so the impulse to succumb to the cynic, victim, or bystander might seem like the only way to go.

The Power of Choice

What we often forget, however, is that we have a secret weapon: choice. The choice is yours, always. No one can take away your power to choose how you react to your circumstances and experience. Any time you try to make it about someone else, you give away your power.

Holocaust survivor Viktor E. Frankl (1905–1997) writes about this powerful idea in his book *Man's Search for Meaning*, published in 1954. Frankl was an Austrian neurologist and psychiatrist who was imprisoned in the Nazi death camps from 1942 to 1945. He lost his wife and both his parents in the concentration camps before he was liberated. In the camps at Theresiendstadt, Auschwitz, and Terkheim (near Dachau), he worked as a doctor, including counseling new prisoners, who were sometimes in such despair that they saw suicide as the only reasonable option. In *Man's Search for Meaning*, Frankl chronicles the most sordid, base, and dehumanizing of environments while proposing that meaning can be found in any existence, even the most brutal and cruel. In the end, he writes, "Everything can be taken from a man but . . . the last of the human freedoms—to choose one's attitude in any given set of circumstances, to choose one's own way." The last freedom we give up is the freedom to choose how we face our circumstances.

The human impulse to give away our power is illustrated time and time again when we work with clients. Remember our example about Sean in chapter 5? One of the questions we asked him—a question we ask almost all our clients—was "What would it take to restore your hope, your willingness to act, and your commitment?" Think about your situation at work or within your family and community. How would you answer that question? What would it take to restore your hope, your willingness to act, and your commitment?

Here are some typical responses:

> "What I want to restore my hope, willingness to act, and commitment is for people to treat me with respect and compassion instead of like some cog in the machine."

> "What I want is for my boss to communicate with me more clearly about what is expected and not expect me to read her mind."

> "What I want is for people to take my input and ideas into account before making important decisions that affect my life."

> "What I want is for my coworkers to stop slacking off and take equal responsibility for doing good work."

Are these desires reasonable? Most people would say they are. But consider the very real ramifications of these kinds of statements. In more than twenty years of asking this question of thousands of people, almost without exception we get the response that people feel their hope, commitment, and willingness to act lie in someone else's hands. How quickly we are willing to give our power and our choice of who we want to be in the world to others, over whom we have no control.

Once that realization is internalized, most people want to take the power back. They want to make a different choice and send out into the world the part of themselves that wants to serve. But while realization and recognition are essential first steps, they often aren't enough when you find yourself immersed in the cynical stew that simmers in most organizations.

Once you choose commitment and hope, it helps to be fortified with ways to confront the cynics/victims/bystanders around you who speak so seductively to the cynic/victim/bystander that will always reside within. We suggest that the best way to start is by engaging a new conversation with those cynics, victims, and bystanders.

This Is My Choice

Long before Maren was leading workshop discussions about the power of changing conversations, she accidentally discovered the power to disarm a cynic. She was the head of the features department at a large metropolitan newspaper during a time of upheaval and radical change that left the staff feeling insecure and resentful. For decades, the newspaper's parent company had produced separate afternoon and morning newspapers, which were viewed as competitors despite their common ownership. Management had decided to merge the two staffs, and except for senior managers, everyone was required to reapply for jobs. When the dust settled, many were in new jobs working alongside people they had previously viewed as the enemy, in a professional sense. The organization's structure was new, processes were unfamiliar, and people were trying to figure out where they fit in. Tension crackled constantly. In the midst of this turmoil, the executive editor made a decision to institute a program that would require everyone to change the way they did their jobs. Department heads, including Maren, were charged with "selling" yet another difficult change to a staff that already felt brutalized.

Although Maren thought the idea might be worth trying, she dreaded the conversation she would have to have with the staff. At a meeting she called to talk about the executive editor's mandate, she looked out at a large group of faces that were sick of the word "change."

As Maren explained the executive editor's initiative, Manny, the staff's most well-entrenched cynic, interrupted with questions and commentary. As he talked, the all-too-familiar fears, disappointment, and cynicism were wafting in the room like the stale, recycled air on an airplane. Maren began refuting his commentary with a combination of logic, pleading, and cheerleading: "Yes, we've been through a lot of difficult changes, that's true, but this change could be good! Yes, other change initiatives have fizzled in the past, but this one has the support of the executive editor. Yes, it is a fact that we're all weary from these changes, but trying this new way of doing things couldn't hurt, could it? Let's be open to it!" As the discussion escalated into a near-argument, it suddenly struck Maren that everything Manny was saying was real and true. She couldn't refute a single thing about his experience. He was citing the perspective of everyone in the room— including her. Everyone on the staff was sick of change, they had seen other change efforts fizzle, and they had been deeply hurt and disappointed by the way they had been recently treated. They once again felt excluded from the decision-making that was going to have a major impact on the way they worked. Maren's efforts to persuade Manny to "get on board" were only intensifying the bad feelings in the room.

So she stopped arguing. She said to Manny, "Look. I hear you. I have been through everything that you have, and I can't deny the truth of what you're saying. You're right. The last thing anyone here wants to tackle is another change that we aren't sure is going to improve the way we do our jobs. But I also believe this could help us do our jobs better, and I am going to give it my best shot. That's my decision. You'll have to decide whether you want to make it work or not. So let's talk about the next item on the agenda." Almost immediately, the tension in the room evaporated.

That is the secret to the new conversation: Let go of persuasion, selling, bartering, convincing. *They do not work.* Make a decision for yourself on where you stand, and when someone tries to tell you how naïve you're being, don't argue. If you are clear about your own choice, you don't need to pour your energies into winning converts. You can simply invite the cynics, victims, and bystanders to make their own choices. That's how it works anyway. Cynicism, helplessness, and lack of commitment are choices we make in response to the circumstances we see—and we can choose something different.

A new conversation for confronting and reframing cynicism looks like this:

1. Restate the other person's position.

2. Ask for acknowledgement that you have it right.

3. Extend understanding and agreement for their position.

4. State your choice for hope and commitment in the face of your own reservations and doubts.

5. Invite the same choice from the other person.

6. End the conversation.

It's not the conversation you're used to having at work, and it will feel awkward and uncomfortable to talk like this at first. This sample conversation gives you an idea of what it might sound like:

> CYNIC: *Have you heard the latest craziness they've come up with around here to make our lives miserable? When are they going to figure it out? These changes they try to shove down our throats never work.*

Listen for understanding. It's extremely difficult (but critically important) to resist the temptation to argue the cynic out of his cynicism. Instead, restate the other person's position, which might sound something like this:

> YOU: *Sounds like you don't have a lot of hope this is going to work. (Or, Sounds like you want a lot more information before you can commit to giving this a try. Or, I hear you saying you don't see how things could ever change around here.)*

Then ask for acknowledgement by saying something like, "Did I get that right?" or "Does that capture how you see things?" If the cynic says no, keep listening and restating until he or she agrees that you have accurately captured what was said. Once that happens, you can begin to extend understanding and agreement. Both parts are important, and it might sound like this:

> YOU: *I know what you are saying. I have doubts about this myself.* [Understanding] *You mentioned the project that failed last year, and you weren't even here five years ago when they tried those other procedures. I remember it well, and it blew up. They brought in a whole new management team after that.* [Agreement]

By acknowledging that you understand the cynic's views and that you also have reservations, and by using your own experiences of disappointment to back up his data, you have made it clear that you see what is at stake and that you honor his legitimate point of view. That's when it's time to state your choice for hope and commitment in the face of your own reservations and doubts. It might sound like this:

> YOU: *Believe me, I've thought through all of these things for myself. And in spite of everything, I am going to do what I can to make this work. In fact, I'm attending the training session to learn more about it.*

After that, invite the same choice. Remember, you're extending an invitation, not looking for an opportunity for persuasion.

> YOU: *So that's the decision I've come to. You'll have to decide for yourself. You could choose to try and make this work, too. It is up to you.*

And then, end the conversation:

> YOU: *So, tell me more about that project you are working on with Sandy's group. (Or, I'm on my way to get coffee. Can I get you some?)*

In having this new conversation, it's important to remember that your purpose is to identify the other person's stance as a choice, not a predetermined outcome. By stating your commitment and inviting the cynic to choose for himself, you make clear the inherent choice to be made. Your goal is not to convince him to change his mind or convert his way of thinking. Trying to persuade someone else to be committed is a sucker's game. It never works.

Watch for this common pitfall. The cynic may say, "Okay, I can see that you're committed. But tell me why you think I should commit to this." What a shiny, juicy, delectable apple has been dangled before you. The cynic is asking to be persuaded, practically begging, actually. This is your big chance, right? He's ripe for conversion!

But biting that apple is a direct path to the sucker's game and will only end up giving you indigestion. It's critical to remember that you can't persuade people to be committed. They must choose. You can say, "I can't tell you why you should commit. You have to determine that for yourself. I am happy to tell you more about why I made the choice I did."

Finally, avoid the trap of making promises, selling, or coercing. Sometimes when you have committed to something, it is easy to become zealous. You can find yourself saying things such as, "I know this will be different, because senior management is behind it." Or "If you commit and follow through, think how good you will feel when we are successful." Or "If you and I can convince just a few others to commit, I know this will work." The danger in making promises, selling, bartering, or trying to coerce is that if the other person ends up disappointed, you've colluded in giving him one more data point to justify his cynicism.

Being a Participant/Observer

Participating in this new conversation, and in others we recommend, means becoming conscious of something you often do unconsciously. It is enormously helpful to develop an awareness of how you act both as a participant and an observer in the moments of conversation.

Conversations happen on three levels simultaneously (see the following figure):

Level 1: The Content Level
Involves: The formal agenda
The difficult news
Unwelcome events
Change projects

Level 2: Other's Emotional Response
Includes concerns about: Loss of control
Facing up to a harsh reality
Being vulnerable

Level 3: Your Emotional Response
Includes concerns about: Loss of control
Competence
Approval
Self-esteem

- The first, surface level is the content of the conversation. It is the subject and the substance of what is being said.

- The second level is the other person's emotional response to the content of the conversation. He or she constantly reacts and makes judgments about what is being said: "right/wrong, good/bad, agree/disagree, willing to/not willing to, work/won't work, happy/sad," and so on.

- The third level is your emotional response to the content *and* to the other's emotional response. You have your own feelings about the conversation's content and you are constantly evaluating the other's response.

To effectively and authentically engage in a conversation, it's helpful to be clear and direct about the content, listen actively, and stay connected. At the same time, it is important to observe what is going on internally and what is going on with the other person. It is like standing outside yourself and observing yourself and the other while you're having the conversation—not easy to do.

You can develop more awareness by noticing what is going on in your head and with your body as you experience emotions connected to the content of the conversation. If you start formulating responses in your mind or constructing rebuttals before the other person stops talking, you're not truly engaged in the content. When you are feeling vulnerable, incompetent, anxious, or reluctant to face a harsh reality, you get cues from your body. Your heart beats faster, your stomach contracts, your muscles tighten. Your fists start to clench or your palms sweat, and you begin squirming in your chair. These are just some of the signals that you are having an emotional reaction. Becoming consciously aware of these signals strengthens the observer in you, and makes it increasingly alert.

Once you develop this awareness, you can begin making conscious choices about whether to act on your emotional response or to let it go. If you notice you're getting defensive, you can choose to stop. If you begin hearing a chorus of "Yeah, but," you can command silence and concentrate on listening and understanding. An effective technique for acting *and* letting go is to say what you are experiencing in the moment using neutral language: "Could you please repeat what you just said? I got distracted, and I want to make sure I am getting this."

The observer has to be able to do two things simultaneously, because you also need to pay attention to the other person's emotional reactions. You can watch for cues such as facial expressions, hand gestures, posture, and other body language. You might notice changes in the tone, volume, or pitch of the voice. Giving voice to what you see, always using neutral language, helps diffuse emotion and refocus the conversation on content:

"I've noticed you're leaning forward and talking much louder. What's going on for you?"

In chapter 11, we'll talk more specifically about tending to the other person's emotional response, especially when it distracts from the issue being discussed.

Attending to all three levels of conversation also means developing better engagement skills. Listening with the intention of understanding is imperative so you can reflect back on what you have heard. Extending understanding means you articulate what you hear and experience based on what the other person says. We recommend using "I" statements when referring to your own emotional responses (Level 3): "I'm feeling defensive about what you're saying, and that's making it difficult for me to listen carefully."

When you talk about what you observe about the other person (Level 2), it's best to use statements that begin with "You seem . . ." or the more neutral "It seems . . ." or "It sounds like . . ." Saying "I understand" is a good-faith attempt at showing empathy, but it is far more powerful to say, "You sound frustrated and concerned that this project is over budget." Or "When I mentioned talking with customers, you frowned and looked a little anxious."

Cynicism, helplessness, lack of commitment, and many other emotional choices are expressed in all three conversational levels, and recognizing them takes practice. As we continue exploring ways to change the conversation, it will become clear how critical the participant/observer skill is to engaging new and authentic conversations.

While it's a lot to pay attention to, the good news is that like everything else, the choice is yours and it gets much easier with time and practice.

Chapter Nine

" Cutting the Ties That Bind "

Adults can be very sentimental about their childhood memories. How easy it was then! No rent to pay, no meals to prepare, on-demand transportation, and free TV. Clean laundry magically appeared in the drawer, someone reminded us to brush our teeth and took us to our dental checkups. Free vacations.

Even if our childhood experiences weren't that idyllic, most of us can relate to the yearning for such an existence. Someone to take care of the details, pay the bills, reassure us that everything will be all right. What a carefree world that would be, right?

But ask a child (particularly one of the teenage variety) for a reality check on how they see their experience. No freedom. Low pay (or no pay) for tasks done and the constant threat of reprisals for not toeing the line. Decisions made without their input and behind closed doors. The constant message from parents, teachers, and other adults, "Trust us. We know what's best. Just do as we say and everything will be all right."

The assumption is that we all grow up to become adults and treat each other in ways that reflect this. But at work, there is often something about the teenager's experience that feels all too familiar. How many managers see parenting as an essential ingredient in successfully managing "their people"? From a practical standpoint, they often see their roles as shielding their employees from the harsh realities of the marketplace and keeping an eye on the "kids" to make sure the work gets done.

The parent–child dynamic in organizations is strong and familiar, and it continues to thrive in corporations, government, and educational institutions everywhere. This is abundantly evident in our conversations, the ways we engage each other, and the processes and policies that establish the confines within which we live.

To be sure, lots of people prefer it that way. How often have you heard someone at work say, "I just want to show up, do my job, keep my head down, and get a paycheck"? Or another common line: "Just tell me what to do and I'll do it." In theory, there's a lot less to worry about when you remain in this child role. If you can say you're not in charge, you can believe it eliminates the need to worry. You believe it absolves you from full accountability and gives you someone else to blame when things go wrong: "I'm not in charge, they are." Many people are reluctant to give up "benevolent parents" because seeing yourself as accountable for the business puts you directly on the hook for its success or failure.

It isn't easy to create a culture where everyone is valued and treated as an adult and chooses the accountability associated with being an adult. Among the first tasks that must be undertaken to create an adult culture is to abandon caretaking as a leadership strategy. It means forsaking the illusion that someone else is responsible for your emotional welfare. It means making a commitment to tell each other the truth. It requires sharing the big picture and opening your eyes to it, even when the news isn't good and the issues are difficult. It requires new conversations that are direct. This can be difficult and demanding, especially in a culture that has never supported those kinds of conversations.

We mentioned in chapter 4 that caretaking is almost impossible to do without a willful dishonesty. Caretaking requires at least two things: (1) that you withhold, change, massage, or obfuscate information and (2) that you choose language for manipulation and effect. You may do this in the name of protecting others, in the way you would protect a child. Whether you are aware of it or not, caretaking is a form of control.

To change the caretaking dynamic, we must all acknowledge its debilitating consequences. We must engage in new conversations that focus on the truth about what's at stake for everyone and the array of choices we have in the present circumstances. Instead of leaders saying, "We are doing everything we can to remedy this situation, just do your job and don't worry—things will be okay," we must begin having conversations that inform others about what is really going on. We must engage in conversations aimed at supporting each other in finding creative solutions for real difficulties.

Remember the manager whose company was reorganizing? People kept coming to him about it, fretting over whether they would lose their jobs. His conversations with them were infused with reassurance as he told them to put their worries aside and just focus on doing their work. "Do the best you can and don't worry about the rest," was his message. We suggested he start a different conversation, one that told people the truth about the company's intentions and put the responsibility for doing something about that on their shoulders. When employees expressed worry about the future at the company, we suggested that the conversation begin like this:

"This business is in a really difficult situation and the uncertainties about our future and jobs are real. My understanding is that the company is planning to downsize. Your job could be at risk and so could mine. Until now, I have seen it as my job to try to make you feel better so you could get through it and maintain job performance. Now I see that has been getting in the way, and I am going to stop. By the same token, you should stop looking to me for protection and reassurance that things will be okay. I can't give you that.

"Here are the choices I see for us. On the one hand, we can be angry, try to withdraw from it, and blame upper management for getting us into this situation. On the other hand, we can get literate about what is going on here. We can begin assessing what skills and competencies are going to be valuable both here and out in the marketplace. My advice is that we take responsibility for learning those new skills rather than waiting for someone to offer them to us. What other choices do you see that we might have under the present circumstances?"

This conversation acknowledges the business reality, frames a few choices, and asks others to think about other choices they may see. This puts the responsibility for dealing with the future squarely on the shoulders of each individual and allows them to respond as adults.

Untangling the Traditional Managing Strategy

As we mentioned in chapter 2, the traditional managing strategy consolidates power at the top of the organization. The five essential elements of organizational power—business literacy, choice, accountability, access to resources, and competency to manage *and* do the work—have historically been concentrated in upper management. In today's world, it doesn't make sense to continue that strategy. Competition is fierce. Those closest to the marketplace and the customers—the people who do the work—must be able to respond quickly and effectively.

A management strategy that distributes organizational power means spreading its five elements out to the furthest reaches of the organization. It almost forces people to stop caretaking each other. It will create a fast, flexible, creative, accountable, and service-oriented workforce and a shared vision for success. It's a big transformation. But every journey begins with small steps, and the beginning steps we suggest address three critical elements of organizational power:

- **Business literacy**, so that everyone in the organization knows "the business of the business," what is at stake, and what their roles are in a successful endeavor. Everyone understands the story the information tells.

- **Choice**, which allows people who are literate about the business to quickly make good decisions in service to the business and customers without having to navigate several layers of bureaucracy.

- **Accountability**, which espouses and supports the notion that people hold *themselves* accountable for the way they engage the business, making good choices in the context of the marketplace and business results, and living openly with the consequences of their actions.

With commitment to a changed strategy, fueled by new conversations, the heavy load of responsibility that has been carried by a few begins to lessen, and power is distributed widely and broadly. This creates powerful individuals in those places where customers experience the business's products and services.

In this chapter we will explore the first two elements, and we will talk about accountability more extensively in chapter 10.

Business Literacy as an Element of Power

It becomes much more difficult to maintain a parent–child culture if the "children" are as well informed as the "parents" about the world in which they operate. If everyone in an organization is educated and literate about what the business stakes are, they don't need to be shielded from its harsh realities. They no longer need to look for someone else to hold them accountable. With widely distributed business literacy, people understand what their roles are in achieving results and are much more likely to take them seriously. Caretaking becomes, in a real sense, anachronistic.

In our consulting work, we encounter a fair share of initial resistance when we talk about the importance of distributing business literacy, especially among executives and managers who have a long history of working in parent–child cultures. When we suggest that sharing their knowledge is essential if they want everyone throughout the enterprise making good business decisions, the frequent reaction is "But they don't really need that information" or "All that information is just going to confuse them" or "They can't handle that information."

Such statements are, of course, the very embodiment of caretaking. They signal a need for executives and managers to examine the way they view people at work. We also advise managers to think about the intentions that underlie that viewpoint. Managers often justify caretaking as being for someone's own good when, at the heart of it, the intention is to avoid dealing with the other's emotional reactions. Often those at the top don't want to deal with the questions and challenges that might arise when people clearly understand the situation. Those in management have to own up to this before they can make changes.

On the other hand, some senior leaders enthusiastically embrace the idea of educating the workforce. They get busy and assign someone in the organization to create a "communications campaign," with posters and charts, company newsletters, and brown bag discussions. In typical executive fashion, they delegate "create business literacy" as a way of checking it off their to-do list. While their intentions are good, by doing this, they absolve themselves from changing their perspectives. More importantly, their day-to-day conversations remain unchanged. While communication campaigns can certainly have value, we don't think they are an effective way of distributing business literacy.

The most practical and powerful way to distribute business literacy is to change, purposefully and with perseverance, the daily conversations about how we work. For the good of the business, we must consciously look for and capitalize on *every* opportunity to share information. We must constantly discover ways to make the operation of the business fully transparent and known to everyone.

Removing the wraps from information about the business is not as complicated as people try to make it, and it is critical to organizational transformation. If people are going to choose accountability and make decisions for the success of the business, they need full disclosure on how the company makes money, how it spends money, what the priorities are, who the competition is, and how well (or not well) the organization is doing in the marketplace.

People need to know everything possible about the environment they're being asked to succeed in. What is their relationship to each other and to other departments in the business? How are they interdependent? What are the strategies that have been chosen to run the business? How are budgets put together? How are costs managed? What is the organization's obligation to its shareholders? What are the most difficult issues the business faces internally and externally?

We also need to explode the assumption that those at "the bottom" are the ones who need to get literate. There is a wealth of untapped information and valuable experience from those who do the core work. They are the closest to the customers, yet their knowledge about how things get done rarely makes its way to the top. What is entailed in doing the core work? How are people thinking about and treating customers and each other? What are the obstacles that keep them from operating efficiently and creatively? What are the difficult issues?

Everyone in the organization needs to discover how things really get done. One client of ours, a medical center in the Southwest, discovered this the hard way when staffing issues became a headache in the radiology department. During the busiest periods in the department, employees were stretched and patient waits were unacceptable. During slack times, employees complained about not having enough to do. The medical center administrator decided changes had to be made. After getting input from the radiology staff, she and her management team set about reworking how scheduling was done.

But when they implemented their changes, things got crazy. When changing employees' schedules, senior leaders had failed to take into account issues such as child care, transportation, and people's preferences for day or night shifts. Rather than raising that difficult issue with the administrator, employees took matters into their own hands. They decided to switch shifts with coworkers so their lives would not be disrupted, but they punched in as the person who had been assigned the original shift. Eventually, someone who was worried about the potential liabilities to the hospital mustered the courage to tell the medical center administrator what was going on. Instead of getting angry, she realized she had been presented a learning opportunity. Her subsequent actions are a wonderful example of the importance of business literacy flowing both ways.

She called a meeting with the management team and radiology employees. Admitting they had bungled the scheduling, she made it clear that switching shifts and checking in as someone else had to stop immediately. She told the staff that she was going to assign scheduling responsibilities to them, but not without constraints. Key measures had to be taken into account. Staffing had to align with the busy and slow times in the department. Patient care had to be a priority. The employees accepted accountability for solving the scheduling problems and were able to accommodate their personal needs.

Through this process, the administrator learned things she hadn't known about how patients flowed through radiology. Certain days of the week had heavier workloads than others, and patient flow was not consistent day to day. She discovered peak times were holidays and the day after holidays, and that the start of the school year also meant more patients. She learned more about the critical interdependencies between emergency room, labs, and radiology and how they affected scheduling. As we watched this change effort, our belief in the importance of distributing business literacy was reinforced. And we had more evidence of the importance of making it a two-way process.

How the business is run should be transparent to everyone involved in running it. Start from the premise that all information is disclosed to all people unless someone can make a solid case why information should *not* be disclosed. Then make that reasoning and argument public.

Creating this kind of transparency will immediately generate new conversations. As people become literate about the business, they will develop a point of view. They will ask difficult questions. This gives everyone ample opportunities to practice new conversation skills: telling the truth, maintaining goodwill, listening, using language for engagement and full disclosure, extending understanding, and dealing with the cynicism, helplessness, and lack of commitment that are the outgrowth of parent–child cultures. We have to learn how to say, "I don't know. Let's find out." We have to address both the questions and the emotional responses associated with honest answers.

A couple of our clients at a large hospital in California took the notion of distributing business literacy very seriously. The hospital was part of a major health care company where the employees were represented by labor unions. The relationship between management and labor had historically ranged from uneasy to contentious to downright hostile. At one time, the relationship had deteriorated to the point where the union was on the brink of a strike. However, both company and labor officials had recognized that a strike or work slowdown could be disastrous for business. After months of negotiation, they entered into a first-of-its-kind agreement that would create a new managing strategy. Under this agreement, management and labor would manage the business as partners.

Tracey, the executive in charge at the hospital, fully embraced the notion of this collaborative management strategy with the labor unions. He and his labor union partner, Alicia, at the time a union representative, both saw distributing business literacy as an essential ingredient in running the business in a partnership environment. They realized it would be necessary to change the way they conversed with each other, and were committed to helping those they worked with do the same.

They began discussing ways they could distribute information more widely and create inclusive deliberation processes. They wanted to ensure that everyone who worked at the hospital had a voice in making business decisions, regardless of what their roles were. The first thing to do, they decided, was to establish monthly meetings involving people from every department and every discipline at the hospital. They designed the meetings to be interactive and solution-oriented rather than to passively share information. About 150 people representing labor, supervisors, and managers from each department were invited to attend the first meeting and would become the regular attendees. (Eventually they instituted a system of rotating membership to create further exposure.)

At the first meeting, Tracey distributed a fifty-page document called "Business Imperatives and Action Plans," which he and his team had spent hours researching and assembling. He then began a new conversation with the 150 employees. "This is what *I* used to worry about," he said, waving the document. "From now on, this is what *we* will be worrying about. Contained in this document is everything we are accountable for and everything we must accomplish this year. I used to keep most of this information to myself, not understanding that you needed it too. The stakes are too high for me to continue holding on to information if we want to be successful."

The document outlined the responsibilities of each department, but Tracey emphasized that individual departments couldn't accomplish their responsibilities without the help of others. The monthly meetings, he told them, were a way for the group to collaborate on decisions in a way that would be better for the business.

"I have been trying to manage this hospital as a collection of independent departments. In reality, we are an interdependent whole that is responsible for delivering high-quality, accessible, and reasonably priced health care," Tracey said. "What happens in the emergency department, for instance, affects six to eight other departments directly and many others indirectly. That's true of every department. It is impossible to manage this complexity from the top. You must begin to do this. We need to have people here who understand what is at stake for our business and how we must deal with it.

"This document is a beginning. It will change, and you will be responsible for identifying changes and bringing them into this plan. You won't understand all of this information at first—some of it I don't fully understand yet. We will figure it out together. For the next two hours, we'll be working in smaller groups so you can begin digesting this information and forming and recording questions you may have about it."

The room stayed silent for a moment, but soon people were buzzing. As they broke into groups, there was a chorus of enthusiastic, energized conversations about the document, the business, and the future. Many new and different kinds of conversations began that day.

People are often reluctant to admit that they don't have all the answers, especially if they have been put in charge. You have to get clear about your own intentions if you are to engage people openly and honestly. Acting on your intentions consistently is necessary to break well-entrenched habits that you may not even realize you have. And you have to be willing to deal constructively with the emotional reaction of others who, for the first time, are being asked to become players after years of being seen as merely doers.

For those steeped in organizational cultures where knowledge is power, the perception of sharing knowledge and giving up power (or the illusion of power) can be daunting and scary. Abandoning caretaking feels like a loss, and one that could put you and maybe the whole organization at risk. Tracey and Alicia realized that the "wait and see" mentality created by caretaking was debilitating to the people they worked with. It was detrimental to business success. Their commitment to continually distributing business literacy and having collaborative conversations forced them to abandon caretaking in their organization. This created more knowledge. Because people throughout the organization were involved, problems were solved more creatively in ways that better served the business.

Keeping new conversations at the forefront of any change effort is a matter of will and intention, not technique and method. Numerous techniques, methods, and processes have been introduced over the years for changing cultures and improving business results. The evidence of the difficulty of true change can be seen in how often these methods are initiated but quickly lose energy. Typically this isn't due to a lack of individual and collective willingness, but to a lack of commitment and consciousness. Things fall by the wayside, which leads to the creation of the "flavor of the month" cynicism that is common today. The only way to combat this is through persistent resolve, dedication, and old-fashioned work.

Choice as an Element of Power

Think about the choices you face every day. Do you choose to wake up on time or hit the snooze button and risk being late to work? One cup of coffee to get going or three, even though you're worried about too much caffeine? How do you feel about the information you read in the newspaper? How will you let it affect the way you see the world? At every moment of every day, you are confronted with myriad choices that affect your actions, feelings, attitudes, and beliefs.

It's no different when you consider the elements of choice that accompany organizational power:

- Choices people make in serving the business

- Choices about the emotional responses people bring to each situation

- Choices people make about their stance when they bring themselves to work

Most of our clients agree that they want people to choose to act like adults at work. They definitely want people to choose service over self-interest (or at least align service with self-interest), and to choose openness, engagement, learning, and contribution.

Yet in a parent–child culture, conversations often don't support what people say they believe. If the organizational culture is going to change, it's critical to be aware of the discrepancies between what you say you believe and how you put those beliefs into action.

Chris Argyris, professor emeritus of business at Harvard University, who has written widely about how individuals and organizations learn, points out that what people in organizations say they want is often belied by the behaviors they exhibit. In his book *Theory in Practice: Increasing Professional Effectiveness* (cowritten with Donald A. Schon), Argyris writes about *espoused theories* and *theories in use*. Espoused theories are your beliefs about how you should and would behave in a given situation: "We believe our employees' number one priority should be our customers' satisfaction." They are the behavioral theories you stand by and give allegiance to.

Theories in use are how you breathe life into your beliefs through the behaviors and conversations you choose. All too frequently in organizations—and in individuals—the two theories don't align. What is especially intriguing about this, as Argyris points out, is that people in organizations collude with this conflict by acting as if it's not occurring.

Seeing this distinction allows you to ask hard questions about the fit between your espoused theories and your theories in use. Many organizations espouse the theory that employees need to take responsibility and should make choices in the best interest of serving customers and, by extension, the business: "Every employee has the responsibility for making sure our customers are satisfied." But how do those in charge react when they disagree with the choices employees make using the best information they have at the time (business literacy) to satisfy a customer? "You made a mistake! That was against policy. You should have checked with me first. Here is what you should do the next time . . ." This is the theory in use.

One way to determine the organizational attitude toward choice is to examine how mistakes are treated. Are mistakes seen as learning opportunities or detriments to success? If mistakes are seen as detriments, something to be avoided, then conversations about mistakes are typically punitive. This creates a culture where the instinctive reaction is to minimize or cover up mistakes, or to shift blame so that true accountability is lost. Honest conversation is quashed because no one wants to get in trouble or embarrass their coworkers. People adopt an attitude of "catch me if you can" or become afraid to act without direction. Punitive treatment of mistakes discourages creativity and the risk-taking that might result in benefits for customers or work processes.

On the other hand, if mistakes are viewed as learning opportunities, as a way to explore what went wrong by challenging assumptions, and if conversations about mistakes are reflective in nature and neutral in tone, we can actually create knowledge. When you change your espoused theory to a belief that mistakes are inevitable and represent an opportunity for expanding knowledge, and you support that through your actions, you have created greater fit between the two theories, as well as a more congruent culture.

Adult cultures have honest conversations about mistakes because we see the value in them. When there is no reason to hide mistakes, more people can be involved in discovering the things that don't work and come up with creative solutions to problems.

Instead of telling someone to "fix this," or fixing it without the benefit of collective knowledge, we can begin to frame choices and ask others to do the same. This stops caretaking because we are honest about what has happened, and we are no longer prescribing or directing others' actions based on our limited views.

Doing this also gets at the heart of accountability. True individual and collective accountability cannot exist in a culture where caretaking is the way of doing business. Caretaking and accountability are antithetical. If I am caretaking you, I'm sending you a message that there is no need for you to be accountable. If I am on the other side of that equation, there are myriad places for me to hide.

We will explore the concept of individual accountability for the whole in the next chapter.

Chapter Ten

" Declaration of Interdependence "

In more than twenty years of doing our consulting work, we continue to hunt for the organization that says, "Our biggest problem is that people are too darn accountable for the success of this business."

Chapter 3 explored the myth of thinking we can hold other people accountable. Being accountable, motivated, and committed is a choice people make, not a mandate with which they comply. We see compliance in others and choose to believe it is accountability. We give compliance to others because we are afraid of our own freedom.

It has been said that the hardest rules to follow are the ones you create for yourself. Choosing accountability for the success of the whole means creating a mindset that says, "I am choosing to be accountable for this business even though there are no guarantees. The future is always uncertain, and I am still going to be accountable."

Organizations have spent many years narrowing the focus of people's accountability at work, sometimes right down to the task level. In the mass production model, individuals repeat the same task hundreds of times per day. In education, teachers teach the same lesson plan year after year. Deviating from the curriculum can have career-limiting repercussions. The common thinking is "I am responsible for my job (as it has been defined for me). If you don't do yours, that's not my problem." Even if people recognize that it *is* a problem, they generally don't see it as their problem to manage. Coupled with the myth of being able to hold others accountable, this narrow focus on jobs, tasks, or roles is a huge contributor to the accountability problem in most organizations.

Let's look at the differences between an organization where the people are showing up to "do my job" (even if they're capable, responsible, and doing it well) and an environment populated with people who see themselves as accountable for the success of the whole business. This is a story about one of our clients, which managed a transformation from the former to the latter.

We worked with an emergency department (ED) at a medical center in a metropolitan area. The medical center was part of a major health care system on the West Coast, and about 80 percent of this hospital's admissions came through the doors of the emergency department. (The rest arrived via doctor referrals, such as preplanned elective or routine surgeries or women having babies.)

The ED was a busy, high-stress operation. It was staffed with competent individuals who genuinely cared about the patients and the business, and the same was true of those who worked throughout the rest of the medical center. However, at the time we began consulting with the company, the ED was struggling with a business-threatening issue that was caused, in part, because individuals didn't see the need to take accountability for the whole. The department was managing its patient flow in a way that was seriously eroding customer satisfaction, quality of care, and the bottom line.

Frequently, the ED became so full that patients were lined up in the halls on gurneys waiting for attention and admission. In extreme cases, some patients were being treated in the halls. Once patients were admitted, there was another long wait to find empty beds for them. Doctors and nurses could not do triage efficiently and effectively in this overcrowded situation. Patients were being subjected to a lack of privacy and intolerable waits when they were physically and emotionally at their worst.

Two things quickly became clear after our initial conversations with those who worked in the hospital. First, admitting a patient was a complex process that required the cooperation and coordination of several departments in addition to the ED—radiology, labs, transportation, environmental services, housekeeping, admissions/discharges, materials management, doctors, and nurses. Second, everyone we talked to, no matter what department, framed this issue as an "ED problem." Except for the medical center executive, no one we talked to in our initial interviews saw themselves as responsible for anything other than what they had been hired and paid to do in their department. The ED patient pileup, they told us, was not something they could influence or control.

It was clear that dealing with these problems was going to require new conversations about issues of accountability, interdependency, and collaboration. The first, most critical conversations involved educating people on what was at stake for the business. As we outlined in the previous chapter, distributing business literacy was a priority. Everyone at the hospital needed to know and understand the circumstances, such as how long patients waited in the ED before they were admitted, how long they waited for required tests and services prior to admission, how long they had to wait for a room after they were admitted, and how long it took to turn over a room after discharge. These issues were influenced by when patients were typically discharged, the time it took to perform tests in the lab or radiology, and the availability of transportation to get patients from one place to another. Peak times of the day or week and many other complex issues also had to be understood.

Everyone also needed to be educated about what this situation was costing the hospital in terms of money, patient outcomes, and patient satisfaction. People had to begin talking with each other across departmental boundaries so they could understand these critical issues and the roles they played. Most importantly, they had to see this as more than the ED's problem. Ignored interdependencies had played a huge role in creating this situation. Finally, people needed to have conversations that would raise their consciousness about what it meant to be accountable for *the whole process* of caring for patients.

In a meeting that included core workers, supervisors, and managers from across the medical center, the ED manager, Elizabeth, began having a different kind of conversation by saying something like this:

> "This problem is out of hand. The quality of our care for admissions, and for those being treated and released, is suffering greatly. Everyone here thinks this is *my* problem. It is not. It is *our* problem. We together are accountable for the whole patient experience because it is through our collective interaction that they get great care or something less. We can't solve this alone in the ED.
>
> "We in the ED have contributed to this difficult situation by being way too protective of our department. We have even discouraged collaboration. We are not going to do that anymore. Some of you may think we are chang-

ing because *our* situation is miserable and we are doing it for ourselves. That is partly true, but much more important is the patient's experience. All you have to do is look at patient satisfaction surveys to see how bad it is. We are all accountable for this. How should we begin to remedy this situation?"

In her introduction to the meeting, Elizabeth started the new conversation with four important elements:

1. She reframed the difficult issues in a way that emphasized the need for every department and every employee to see themselves as being accountable for the entire patient experience. She helped people understand that it was their collective efforts, not the work of individual departments, that comprised the patient experience.

2. She owned her contribution to the problem by admitting she had protected her turf and had discouraged collaboration.

3. She acknowledged she couldn't resolve this critical business issue alone and she needed everyone's help.

4. She shifted responsibility for coming up with a plan—or at least the first steps of a solution—to others in the meeting. In this way, she clearly signaled her intention to collaborate *and* share the accountability.

We'd love to report that her speech produced rousing enthusiasm and a crowd that jumped to its feet, fists pumping, while shouting, "Let's go out and win one for the Gipper." But this was the real world, not Hollywood. The employees' immediate reaction was defensive. They began ticking off all the reasons they couldn't possibly be accountable for the whole of the patient experience. They saw themselves as accountable for the patient experience only when the patient was in their hands, and after the "handoff," the patient was someone else's problem.

Panel conversations were conducted with patients, and patient satisfaction surveys were reviewed. Conversations slowly began to change. People stopped saying things like "It's not my job," but continued to have the attitude that "if *they* would do better, this wouldn't be such a big problem." The resident cynics, victims, and bystanders added their voices to the chorus. People became even edgier with each other, and it was reflected in the patients' experiences at the hospital, though no one seemed to want to acknowledge that was the case.

We noticed another problem. When people convened to talk about the issues, conversations were fragmented because information was fragmented. Departments or groups within departments were meeting without essential information or input from those whose collaboration was necessary to resolve the problem. These meetings were important and, to an extent, useful. But they were also a symptom of how lack of information contributes to lack of accountability for the whole. Meetings were reflecting the cultural beliefs about the importance of individual accountability versus accountability for the good of the entire business. Without the input of other departments and without information being distributed throughout the organization, the impact of these types of meetings was severely limited.

We had to figure out a way to get the members of the whole talking to each other to find real and lasting solutions. We began working with Elizabeth and others to change the forums in which they were having conversations. Large group deliberation sessions were held where information was exchanged and decisions could be made with broader input. In these meetings, people discovered none of the individual departments was exclusively the source of the problem. Within departments, work quality was high, employees were working efficiently, and most were on target within the financial budget. It was clear that the breakdown was "in the white space between the departments," the no-man's land where no one had specific, assigned accountability. For instance, sometimes patients were left on gurneys in the hallway outside a lab or other department waiting to be "discovered" by whoever was supposed to care for them next.

"Simple," people said, "we'll just appoint someone to make sure people or departments are accountable in the areas where no one, at least on paper, is responsible for the patient." But as the large group focused on what it meant to be accountable for the whole, they realized that making those kinds of assignments would only add more layers to the process that was causing accountability problems in the first place.

Fear also had to be confronted. Managers saw the notion of accountability for the whole as an erosion of their authority and (illusion of) control, a ceding of the responsibilities they had for managing their departments and the people who worked in them. Core workers were reluctant to take on what they saw as a management responsibility, which they argued was outside their job descriptions and salary ranges.

But as the conversations began centering on patient care and the experience of their customers, a slow realization began coalescing the group. Patients, most of whom were in distress or serious pain, didn't care about the in-fighting among departments and what was "fair." They didn't care if doing something that could make them feel better and more secure wasn't in the job description of those working in nonmanagement positions. Patients needed whoever was taking care of them to have the information, authority, and accountability to resolve issues that would make their experience as seamless as possible.

This meant the group had to come up with ways to change the conversations so that workers on the ground could raise and resolve difficult issues quickly, without constantly going up and down the chain of command. They needed to find ongoing ways to deliberate across department boundaries to find solutions for problems in a daily, time-efficient way, then quickly disseminate the information that came out of those meetings.

After several months, hospital workers began seeing changes that had been effected by their new ways of perceiving accountability. The number of patients in the halls shrank. The lag time for patient admissions was reduced. Patients were moved into their rooms more quickly, and the time it took to turn around a room for the next patient decreased significantly. Knowledge of how each department affected the whole and the development of processes that allowed speedy resolutions to problems meant a far different experience for their patients. As a result of the collaborative work methods, patient satisfaction ratings began to improve significantly.

The different points of view regarding patient issues didn't go away. But the framework for thinking about how to resolve those issues had been altered dramatically. Hospital workers focused more on patient care and less on personal or departmental convenience. They recognized that there wasn't a single employee at the hospital who was not accountable for the whole of the patients' care experience.

In large organizations with many departments and scores of employees, the idea of seeing yourself as accountable for the whole can seem daunting or even ludicrous. "I can't possibly be accountable for something this big! I am not that powerful, and there are too many variables outside my control." But being accountable does not mean always having your own way. Nor does it mean that no one is in charge. True accountability asks you to recognize that the contributions you make as an individual affect the whole enterprise. Keep that at the forefront of everything you do.

Choosing accountability for the whole and working in partnership are the same thing. By reframing your view to include the reality that each individual—and every department—is your partner, you acknowledge that partners are people who choose to be accountable for each other's success. Partners are people who tell each other the truth, talk openly about doubts and difficult issues, openly acknowledge when things are not working, and extend understanding and forgiveness.

Let's see what this looks like at the individual level.

Being Accountable to a Community

We have a friend who recently was involved in a business reorganization where some people were let go, some were offered early retirement packages, and everyone else had to reapply for their jobs. People were assigned to teams, and employees were told that working for the team was the new way of doing business. However, neither the organization's policies and procedures nor the evaluation system had been altered. Our friend told us, "Everything about my job—my performance evaluation, my pay, my assignments—is based on what I do as an individual. That actually puts me in competition with others on my team. But they're telling us that if we want to be successful at this company, we have to be team players. It's a contradiction."

Her comment described an organizational culture that espoused accountability for the whole but failed to see how its practices undermined that goal. There was a serious conflict between espoused theories and theories in use.

Performance evaluations are a typical example of how organizations' espoused theories are contrary to their theories in use. The organization says it wants employees to behave as though they are important members of the team and accountable for its success. Yet elaborate procedures have been designed to hold people accountable as individuals, including tying compensation to their individual performance. It's sending the message that without individual performance evaluations, no one would be accountable and the place would fall apart.

Imagine, if you can, how the typical conversation surrounding a performance evaluation might sound in another arena of life. A woman, remembering that the next day is her wedding anniversary, turns to her husband at breakfast and says,

> "Honey, can you believe that tomorrow we will have been married eight years? Happy anniversary! You know what that means, right? It is time for your annual performance review!
>
> "What I'd like you to do today is sit down and reflect on things you have done particularly well this year as my husband and the father of our children. Then I'd like you to make a list of the things you did not do so well and outline areas where you could improve. While you're doing that, I'll be making a list of your accomplishments this year, and developing ways I think you could improve your performance next year. I'll look at our yearly plan and decide whether you've met the goals of our household.
>
> "Once we've discussed this year's overall performance, I will give you a final rating that will help me decide whether or not to increase your yearly entertainment allowance. If you score well, we might be able to take an extra vacation this year. If your score hasn't improved over last year, we may have to look at probation. And if that doesn't improve things, our marriage could be in jeopardy."

It is a laughable scenario, right? Adults don't manage their relationships like that. And yet most of us meekly submit to a process that, at its heart, tells us we won't choose to be accountable or committed unless someone or something forces us to. Setting goals, being accountable for them, and understanding the consequences of failing to be accountable are important. In fact, they are essential. But in adult cultures, responsibility for performance should rest with the individual.

We propose a new performance evaluation conversation that we call "Doubts, Promises, and Consequences." It could replace the traditional annual performance evaluation (more about this in "A Practical Guide to Authentic Conversations" at the end of the book), and it could also be used at the beginning of a project or assignment, or when a new initiative is being launched. You can have this conversation with a project team or another group to which you see yourself accountable. It has five elements:

1. Talk about the doubts you have about the project or situation, your ability to contribute, and potential difficult issues.

2. Talk about your strengths and abilities, realistically assessing the contributions you can make to a successful outcome.

3. Ask for feedback from others about your doubts and assessments. Ask the group to share *their* doubts about your ability to contribute.

4. Make specific promises for performance results.

5. Choose realistic consequences for nonperformance.

A conversation with these elements might sound something like this:

> "Thanks for joining me today at the beginning of this project, which is important for this unit and the company.

You are important to me and to the success of this project. I have a few doubts and concerns and want to talk about some of the difficult issues I see. First, this project will require cooperation with other departments, one of which we've historically had a difficult relationship with. As a team, I don't think we have always worked as well with other departments as we could have. Also, I'm not as familiar as I'd like to be with the technology we'll be using. That makes me nervous, and given my inexperience in that area, I wonder about my ability to contribute.

"Another thing that concerns me is that when things have gone wrong in the past, I've responded by being defensive and edgy with team members and other departments. This type of project is not my favorite kind, so I'm also a little worried about maintaining my commitment and enthusiasm.

"On the other hand, I do have solid organizational skills, which is a strength we will need, and I learn quickly and can apply what I learn. I also really want to support this team, and I'm committed to making this business as successful as possible. Dana, perhaps you could talk about the doubts you have about this project and my ability to contribute."

After doubts and difficult issues have been raised and discussed, and it is clear what strengths and skills will be contributed, promises about the outcomes to be delivered are made. The group has a critical responsibility to listen and react as the "voice of the business." This helps everyone in the conversation keep the focus on accountability for the good of the whole.

"Here are the promises I am willing to make to you for this project: I will manage my edginess and anger so they don't get in the way, and I want you to tell me in the moment if I am not doing this. I will learn all I can about the technology in the next two weeks by meeting with engineering, systems, and marketing so I am prepared. I will continue to meet with them and others throughout the project so I don't slow us down. I will use my organization skills and project management tools to keep us on track. And lastly, I will do everything I can to maintain my enthusiasm and commitment for this project until it is successfully completed. I also need your help in telling me directly if you notice that I have lost enthusiasm or commitment. Do these sound like promises you need from me?"

The group then responds to these promises. They may ask questions, make suggestions, ask for different or additional promises, and so on. The group negotiates, reaches agreements, and writes the promises down.

The final part of the conversation deals with consequences you choose and are willing to accept if you do not deliver on your promises. The underlying assumption is that as part of accountability, you understand the consequences for nonperformance. One set of natural consequences for nonperformance is related to the diminished success of the project that you manage together as a group. In this conversation, the individual chooses consequences for himself or herself.

"Recognizing that this is important work and that I am a key member of the team, I have chosen two consequences I would expect if I don't follow through on my promises. First, if I am unable to keep us on track and on time or keep you appropriately informed of schedule changes, I won't manage another project until you are satisfied that I have improved my skills in this area. Second, if I can't learn the technology well enough to fully contribute to the team and satisfy our customer, I will go to the customer and own up to my shortcomings and figure out concrete ways that this won't happen again. I am not sure what those are right now, but I trust we can figure it out if necessary. Do these consequences sound reasonable to you?"

Consequences are also negotiated, and the group can help make sure that these are not so unreasonable that they smack of "falling on my sword." The point is to give the promises some heft for reasons of partnership. In adult cultures, choice is real. People understand what is at stake and make choices that mean something. They are willing to acknowledge, and live publicly, with the consequences associated with their choices.

In our emergency department story, people eventually realized that their patients lived with the consequences of their individual and collective choices about accountability. They also understood that in a highly competitive marketplace, the patients' experience was key to keeping customers and gaining new ones.

Choosing accountability for the whole means awakening yourself to something that has always been true: you cannot be successful alone. If you acknowledge that, you need to start examining all the practices, policies, procedures, and work processes that contradict the truth that we are all accountable for business success. If they don't support that truth, why continue using them?

Accountability is an individual issue and also a systems issue. As individuals, we must begin to acknowledge our contributions and consciously act in ways that are congruent with the notion of being responsible for the success of the whole. Systemically, we must create ways of governing and working in support of this reality. Moving consciously in this direction allows us to stop spending so much time, energy, and resources on trying to figure out better ways to do the impossible—hold others accountable.

Chapter Eleven

" Open Season–Remove the Camouflage! "

Steven, a vice president of human resources at a large hospital, came rushing through the outer office where his secretary sat. He shook Jamie's hand quickly and continued briskly into his office for their long-scheduled meeting. As they began to talk about some of the difficult issues the hospital was experiencing, Steven shuffled through stacks of paper and files on his desk and credenza. A few moments later, his phone rang. Steven answered, had a brief conversation, and then hung up. Jamie reengaged the conversation regarding the hospital. As he continued talking, he watched Steven open his desk drawer, extract shoe polish and a rag, remove his tasseled loafers, and begin polishing!

When we tell this story at workshops, most participants are appalled. They comment on the rudeness of Steven's actions. That is one way of looking at it, to be sure, but Jamie uses this story to illustrate two things that can get in the way of authentic conversations: not paying attention to what is going on in the moment, and taking things personally.

Three specific actions signaled to Jamie that Steven was not fully engaged and focused on their conversation. Jamie called them out: "Steven, you really seem distracted. You were in a hurry coming in today, you have been looking for something on your desk while we've been talking, and you interrupted our conversation to take a phone call. Now you are polishing your shoes. Tell me what is going on with you."

Steven's look of relief was instant and obvious. He said, "I'm sorry. I have a budget meeting with my boss after this, and I'm worried because we are over budget at a time of budget cuts. I am afraid it's not going to go very well. These meetings are always difficult for me."

What Jamie recognized in the situation was specific behaviors that were distracting from the content of their meeting. They decided together that Steven's emotional state over the upcoming budget meeting was a distraction that was making it difficult to focus on their meeting. They decided to reschedule.

In chapter 8, we diagrammed how conversations occur on three levels simultaneously—the content level, the other's emotional response, and your emotional response (see page 108). Attending to all three levels is critical to successfully managing conversations. Doing this allowed Jamie to recognize that something was getting in the way of the content of Steven's and his conversation. When this happens, it is resistance.

Defining Resistance

People in organizations must constantly manage difficult and unwelcome changes, unwanted mandates, and other demands that emerge in unexpected ways. Groups or individuals faced with these circumstances are going to have strong feelings, particularly when the changes affect or threaten them. None of us typically welcomes circumstances that make us feel vulnerable, force us to face harsh realities, or diminish whatever control we think we have over our lives and destinies. Work *is* personal. Fear, confusion, and anger are normal responses to perceived threats, but rarely are these reactions expressed openly and directly.

Resistance is defined here as a *camouflaged* or *indirect* expression of an underlying emotional concern, usually stemming from worries about loss of control, vulnerability, or facing a difficult situation. It's important to note that when emotional concerns are expressed directly, that is not resistance. When people openly disagree, it is just that—open disagreement—and therefore not resistance.

In his book *Flawless Consulting*, Peter Block writes,

> The key to understanding the nature of resistance is to realize that the resistance is a reaction to an emotional process taking place within. . . . It is not a reflection of the conversation we are having with the [other] on an objective, logical, rational level. Resistance is a predictable, natural, emotional reaction to the process of being helped and (or) against the process of having to face up to difficult organizational problems.

Forms of Resistance

Resistance can prevent individuals and organizations from successfully navigating change, reaching important decisions, resolving problems, or facing difficult situations. It occurs in the course of the meetings we attend and in the daily conversations we have with one another.

Upon hearing painful or unwelcome news, few of us directly acknowledge the difficult feelings that result. We tend to express our fear, concern, or anger indirectly in ways such as these:

- Going silent

- Changing the subject

- Giving superficial compliance

- Questioning competence or credentials

- Getting lost in irrelevant details

- Asking for more detail

- Denying or smoothing over the difficult reality

- Blaming others

- Claiming confusion

- Getting angry

- "Killing the messenger"

- Giving one-word answers

- Rambling

- Jumping to conclusions

- Appealing to the other's self-interest

These types of responses and many others express indirectly or camouflage concerns, fears, and vulnerabilities. They distract attention from the content of a conversation and make it extremely difficult to focus on the issue. That is the point of resistance—to put off or avoid dealing with a harsh reality.

Resistance happens on the second and third levels of a conversation, not on the content level. In fact, the emotional responses often distract from the content. Though everyone has experienced it, resistance is not often seen clearly in the moment. One of the best ways to develop the skill of recognizing resistance is to discover the ways you do it yourself and learn how to express *your* underlying concerns directly. Instead of going silent, changing the subject, or attacking the messenger, for instance, you can say, "This change is far-reaching and it looks like it could affect my job. The uncertainty scares me." Or "This is a huge change for me and the role I have played. I am worried that I won't be good at what I am supposed to do." The point is to put into words what you are experiencing and feeling, and manage yourself in the conversation so your emotional issues do not distract or get in the way.

Dealing with Resistance

Dealing with resistance in others is an equally demanding skill. You have to recognize it, decide when to confront it, and then learn effective ways of calling out the resistance and refocusing on the content. *Ignoring resistance never makes it disappear*—it persists and usually gets stronger until it is confronted.

The purpose of dealing with resistance is to get the conversation back on track so that everyone can focus on the content, or to explicitly change the conversation's content to something that is relevant and clear to all. It is not therapy. Nor is it an attempt to persuade someone to feel differently or get over their feelings—that is just a form of caretaking. The goal is to get a direct expression of underlying emotions, concerns, or reservations, which will help everyone better focus on the content of the conversation. Addressing resistance requires three actions: identify the resistance, choose connection and goodwill, and decide what to do about it.

Identify the Resistance

If a behavior distracts from the content of a conversation two or three times, treat it as resistance. At the first appearance of potential resistance, respond in good faith. For example, if someone asks, "What background do you have for leading this change?"

answer the question with goodwill. If the person then goes silent, you can treat it as "thinking behavior." But the third time a distraction to the content occurs, recognize it as resistance and address it. If the behavior is so disruptive that the conversation can't continue, confront the behavior immediately.

Choose Connection and Goodwill

In the face of difficult behavior, it is challenging to summon up goodwill and extend yourself to someone. But it is essential to stay connected. Anger, placating, lecturing, or counterattacks won't overcome resistance, they will strengthen it. Your feelings in the moment aren't the point here. You must focus on getting the conversation back on track.

We are not recommending that people be allowed to be abusive. However, focusing on what you are trying to accomplish with the content can help you remember your intention. Another's emotional reaction typically does not have anything to do with the person delivering the content, so it is important that you try not to take it personally. The emotional responses that characterize resistance have to do with harsh realities, vulnerability, fear, and perceived loss of control. If you are unable to confront the underlying emotional concern without choosing connection and goodwill, it is better to delay the conversation.

Decide What to Do About It

It is important to show support for the individual by understanding the difficulty he or she is experiencing. You can display this understanding in your tone of voice, eye contact, facial expression, and other body language that is compassionate and engaging. Confronting the behavior requires using direct language and as few words as possible, and getting quickly to the point in a nonjudgmental way. When the underlying concern is expressed directly, extend understanding and agreement to show support and validation. Once this has been done, return to the content level of the conversation.

This could become manipulative if you're not clear about your intentions. Supporting, confronting, and dealing with resistance are techniques that can be applied with intent to engage or intent to manipulate. If people feel manipulated, it is probably a sign that you should pay more attention to what your intention is in the moment.

The Progression of Dealing with Resistance

When receiving difficult news, talking about change, or dealing with a mandated project, it's likely that people will respond with resistance. Their feelings are legitimate and need to be aired. An unspoken reservation can create future problems and block an individual or group from getting on with its work.

Sometimes good-faith statements aren't enough to return people to the content level of a conversation. The following diagram shows a progression for confronting resistance until it becomes necessary to consider whether or not to continue with the conversation, relationship, or project. Levels 1 and 2 are easily integrated into any conversation by asking questions or making statements. Levels 3 and 4 are designed to process how you are engaging each other over the conversation's content.

LEVELS FOR DEALING WITH RESISTANCE

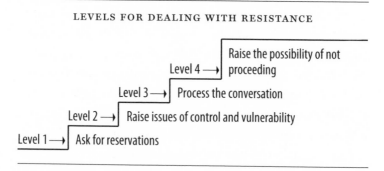

Level 4 → Raise the possibility of not proceeding

Level 3 → Process the conversation

Level 2 → Raise issues of control and vulnerability

Level 1 → Ask for reservations

Level 1: Ask for Reservations

Remember, it is important to deal with your own resistance first. Therefore it is important to state your reservations openly, put into words what you are experiencing, and support the legitimacy of everyone's reservations. If others do not initially raise their reservations, ask for them directly with goodwill and compassion, in a way that makes it clear you want to hear the truth. After dealing with the first reservation, ask for others. Continue to ask until you are reasonably certain all the reservations have been aired. After working through the reservations, test the willingness of the individual or group to return to the content of the conversation.

Here are ways you might ask for reservations:

"How's this going for you?"

"What reservations do you have?"

"What other concerns do you have?"

"That was a worthwhile discussion. Before we go on, what other reservations do you have?"

Level 2: Raise Issues of Control and Vulnerability

It is important to state directly what is getting in the way of the conversation's content. *Describe, don't judge.* For example, when Jamie was speaking to Steven, he didn't say, "You have been inattentive and rude since we started, and it's clear that I am wasting my time talking to you." That type of statement is a judgment and is likely to lead to defensiveness and more difficulty. Instead, Jamie described the behaviors he saw: "Since we started talking, you have been in a hurry, distracted by papers and the phone, and now you are polishing your shoes." The key is to keep your statements simple and to the point. Don't go into great detail. Don't offer explanations. Things you could say include:

> "It looks as if we are spinning our wheels. I keep asking the same questions and you are responding with silence or one-word answers."

> "It's difficult to continue when people constantly interrupt and change the subject."

Then ask for acknowledgement, which could sound something like this:

> "It seems like you are angry or disappointed or worried about the changes I have presented. Am I on target? Tell me what's going on."

After confronting the behavior, shift the responsibility for proceeding to the other person. After confirming and airing the concerns, ask questions to determine whether the individual or group is ready to return to the content of the conversation:

> "I want to figure out the best way to respond to the changes. Where do you want to go from here?"

> "I'd like to get us refocused and on topic. What do you suggest we do next?"

> "It's important for me to know if you are disappointed. I am a little disappointed too. How do you want to proceed?"

Continue processing the conversation and keep in mind the goal is to get the underlying emotional concern expressed, *not to resolve it*. If people continue to feel stuck and you are feeling powerless or about to give up, it is a signal that it's time to move to the next level.

Level 3: Process the Conversation

If the conversation is going so badly that the content is getting lost, it is critical to talk about what is happening. Describing what is going on in an empathetic, compassionate, and authentic way can be a powerful means for refocusing. At this level, the decision is to:

- **Explicitly stop the conversation and change the content:**

  "Let's stop. I feel like we're stuck."

  "Let's take a time out. It feels like we've hit a wall."

- **Briefly recap the original goal for the conversation or meeting:**

  "My intention was to tell you about a difficult situation and enlist your help in how we are going to respond to it."

  "The purpose of this meeting was to tell you about a new work process that will affect our jobs, and work with you to iron out potential problems."

- **Describe what has happened that resulted in things getting off track:**

  "Since we started this conversation you've been silent or attacking me, and now you are assigning blame."

  "This conversation has had constant interruptions since I described the new process. It has made it difficult to focus on the topic."

- **Name *your* contribution to the problem:**

  "I've been spending way too much time defending my position, and now I'm starting to agree with anything you say just to get through this moment."

"My responses to your questions have become defensive. I can feel myself getting irritated and that's not helping."

- **Name the underlying concerns and admit you are at an impasse:**

  "It seems like you're upset and worried that I think you were the cause of this difficult situation, and it feels like we're not getting anywhere."

  "My guess is that we are all upset, scared, or angry about the impact this is going to have on us, and it feels like we are stuck."

- **Make a good-faith statement of positive intention and directly ask for help:**

  "I want us to figure out how we can resolve this difficult issue, but I can't do it alone. I need your help."

  "My intention is to work with this group to find the best way to proceed in the face of this news. We need to help each other. I can't do this on my own."

- **Shift the responsibility back to the individual or group:**

  "Where do you want to go from here?"

  "How do you want to proceed?"

Finally, and this can be a very difficult thing to do, *be silent* until you get a response. Silence allows others to reflect on the situation and what you have said. Silence may feel uncomfortable, but talking now will prevent others from processing the conversation. If several moments pass and the silence feels intolerable, say something like:

"I don't know what to make of your silence."

"It's difficult to read your silence."

Level 4: Raise the Possibility of Not Proceeding

Sometimes no matter how hard you try, things become so difficult that it may be necessary to discuss the possibility of not proceeding with the conversation, relationship, or project. If you feel you've explored every option and haven't found a way to productively continue the conversation or meeting, be willing to discuss the possibility of terminating it. When you present the option of ending the conversation or meeting, be sure it is not framed as a forgone conclusion, a subtle manipulation, or an outright threat. Though emotions are likely to be high, emphasize authenticity, connection, goodwill, and honesty:

> "I think we ought to look at the possibility of ending this conversation [or, not proceeding with this project]. We seem to be going over the same points again and again. I think we are stuck. What do you think?"

> "This meeting seems to have stalled. It feels like we're arguing rather than discussing, and I think it's time to talk about ending it for now."

Name the behaviors you've seen in the individual, group, and yourself that are getting in the way. Ask for a viewpoint about not proceeding:

> "It looks like I am trying to force a discussion that you don't feel ready to have, and I am feeling frustrated and a little out of control. What would happen if we postponed this conversation?"

"I've been getting defensive, and you appear angry about the way this is going and how it might affect you. Let's talk about the risks involved in not doing this right now."

Finally, come to an agreement on whether, or how, to proceed.

Using these new conversations to deal with resistance and talking about underlying concerns might feel uncomfortable at first, even scary. These skills aren't employed in parent–child relationships because the power roles are clear, compliance is the rule, and underlying concerns are not considered relevant to getting things done. People are not accustomed to talking in this way. And yet the fact remains we are emotional. We don't leave our hearts at the door, especially when we care about something. Beginning to honestly talk about our emotions and dealing with them openly honors what we all know is there anyway.

By mustering authenticity and compassion, you bring into the room a part of yourself that parent–child relationships have desperately tried to deny. Dealing with resistance in yourself and in others is taking the adult route and choosing accountability for the success of the conversation.

Conclusion

" Starting the Revolution "

Maren loved the birthday card she found several years ago for her younger sister. It made her laugh then, and today it resonates with this book's theme of personal accountability. On the front of the card, along with a cartoon illustration of two girls, were these words: "Sister, as kids we called each other names, picked on each other, and competed for Mom and Dad's attention. Now that we're grown-ups, it is time for us to treat each other with love, dignity, and respect."

Inside the card was this message:

"You go first."

One of the dilemmas in writing this book was addressing the difficult issue of starting the revolution. When we conduct our workshops on how to change culture through authentic conversations, it seems that the right people are never in the room. If we're working with a group of leaders, they say, "This would be great for our employees! We need to get them in here." If the room is full of core workers, they want to know if management has attended this workshop, because "We can't do this unless *they* do, and they aren't doing it now." Another question that frequently gets asked is "How can we change the conversation if *they* don't?" Sometimes it is a simple statement: "This won't work here because the organization isn't ready for it." These questions and statements, and others like them, have a subtext in common: "You go first."

Do we think leaders should be out in front, taking accountability for transforming their organizations by changing the conversations to create adult cultures? Yes, we do. Danah Zohar, who coauthored the book *Spiritual Capital* with Ian Marshall, points out, "It is a well-known sociological law that a 10 percent minority in any culture begins to unsettle and change that culture." She posits further that if 2 to 5 percent of the top leadership in an organization undergoes profound personal transformation, and another 10 percent of their direct reports eventually join them on the journey, "The culture will have a leadership profile sufficient to raise the motivational level of the whole organization. . . ." Like Zohar and Marshall, and many, many others, we believe that critical connections are made when a relatively small number of people shift their views and behavior. The more critical connections made, the more powerful the impact on organizational culture.

But we want to be emphatic about this: The revolution begins with the person in the mirror. It begins with you, regardless of the type of work you do, where you sit, how much you make, your title, or the size and location of your office. Much like the answer we advocate for the question "Who is accountable for the success of this business?" our answer to "Who starts the conversation revolution?" is "I do."

One could interpret what has been written on these pages as self-help, pop psychology, a collection of great techniques to help people through difficult moments, or steps for getting better business results. In the authors' minds, there is something else that goes much deeper than that, and it is difficult to write about because it is so personal. It has to do with worthiness, purpose, humility, fear, anxiety, and facing the fact that it is up to you to create the world you want to live in, here and now, with the people in this room. It is about letting go of the wish that someone else will make it easier, pave the way, or take responsibility for you and your circumstances. If you can't do these things, you will never be able to say, "I will go first."

Dealing with this transformation is about focusing on intention, which we discussed in chapter 7. Getting clear about who you want to be in the world requires deep humility, honest introspection, and constant attention to developing self-awareness. One of our favorite quotes, attributed to the late British thespian George Arliss, speaks to this: "Humility is the only true wisdom by which we prepare our minds for all the possible changes of life." Through genuine, deep reflection, you are better equipped to confront uncomfortable truths about yourself. You are more prepared to shed unconscious assumptions about who you are, who others are, and what we want to create or accomplish together. In a scene from the 1995 film *Don Juan de Marco*, Johnny Depp's character, whose sanity is being questioned, tells the psychiatrist played by Marlon Brando, "There are only four questions of value in life: What is sacred? Of what is the spirit made? What is worth living for? And what is worth dying for?"

One way to get clearer about your intention is to invest significant, reflective time finding your own answers to questions such as these:

- Who do I want to be in this world?

- What is my purpose?

- What am I trying to create?

- What contributions do I want to make?
- What legacy do I want to leave?

When you develop satisfying answers to these questions, the decisions about how you live out your intentions become more relevant, illuminating, and authentic. Your determination to act in a certain way becomes firmer. That is where authentic conversations start, and that is where your work truly begins.

No moment is quite so unsettling and anxiety-provoking as when you face yourself and ask, "Am I prepared to live in the world as an adult? Do I have the necessary courage and determination to live in a world where I truly understand that others are not responsible for my sense of belonging, my sense of security, and my happiness? Am I prepared to face the mirror, lock eyes with myself, and say, 'I have only one person to look to for creating my life and my world, and that is me'"?

The moments spent wrestling with these issues are daunting. You feel fragile. You would rather turn to anyone in the world other than yourself to find answers. The demand to be accountable for your life and what you accomplish in your lifetime seems enormous, out of proportion. The resources of your heart and mind seem so scarce, so difficult to unearth. No one wants to feel scared or anxious. At these times it is seductive to contemplate a more comfortable life, one where you see others as responsible for your future.

Falling back into old patterns, being the parent or being the child, seeking safety, security, and a sense of well-being outside of yourself—those choices are always available. We all know how to live in that old groove very well. You can be there in less than a heartbeat. All you have to do is turn away from the person you want to become.

In some of his writings, Joel Henning, Jamie's late partner and dear friend, put it like this:

If I keep my face in this new direction, I will experience the anxiety, starkness, and loneliness that come from taking that position. What the universe silently leaves in my hands is the answer to the following questions: "Does turning this new way give me a sense of purpose, authenticity, and meaning? If taking this new position at home or in the workplace will not give me comfort, will it give me a sense of more fully being what I should be?"

If I want to live a life that doesn't end in disappointment, anger, and bitterness, where I don't see myself constantly taking care of other grownups and trying to be responsible for them, and where comfort and security are not my ultimate values, I must turn toward this new choice. I have to stop seeing myself as a child who is controlled by others and cease longing for the comfort of knowing it is someone else's fault when things go awry. The universe is silent on these issues and the silence is deafening.

Yes, this does have business implications. Yes, it will make a difference in how organizations operate in the marketplace. Our experience shows us these connections are explicit and clear. But in the long run, what is most important is each person's willingness to continuously make the choice to create purpose and meaning in a life he or she can believe in.

Turning in this new direction, each of us becomes willing to be the voice of the business. We reach deep within and summon the courage to develop an independent point of view, raise difficult issues, choose for goodwill, stay humble enough to be influenced by others, and cling to hope and optimism in the face of disappointment. We care about others' success as much as our own. We seek collaboration, not victory.

These become the foundation of our future conversations as we deliberate the issues of the business and choose personal accountability for its welfare and success. These conversations replace the caretaking, promising, prescribing, bartering, and demanding conversations that have characterized so many of our relationships in the workplace. We become willing to forsake our perceived safety and security and replace them with doing what is honorable, ethical, and right. *We do it because this is who we want to be in the world.*

One way to make these intentions real and visible is to go public, not with an artificial "statement of values," but by sincerely engaging others in what you want to create. An explicit expression of your visions and intentions helps you hold *yourself* accountable. It tells the world, "This is who I want to be, this is what I want to stand for. Please hold me accountable for this." You also invite others to give feedback when your actions and intentions are incongruent. This sets the stage for a powerful personal transformation and full, rich, authentic conversations.

Such a transformation will not happen overnight. But it can begin today. For those who are clear about their intentions and want to begin the journey, one approach we suggest is beginning with the commitments outlined in chapter 7. Choose one to focus on for a month. If you choose the commitment "recognizing others as free and accountable," as an example, spend time thinking about how you would live it out. Questions you might want to reflect on include:

- How have I traditionally viewed people at work? At home? In general?

- What are the ways I try to hold others accountable?

- How do I expect others to hold me accountable?

- What does "holding others accountable" look like where I work?

- What do I need to be aware of and pay attention to while living this commitment?

- What situations might make it more challenging?

- What do I need to change about myself to start seeing others as free and accountable and living this out with them?

- What are the concerns, doubts, or reservations I have about myself in making this change?

After reflecting on these questions, you can begin to create a "formulating intention." This is an intention that embodies the change to which you are committing. An example using this commitment could be "I will engage others by emphasizing their freedom of choice, and I will confront issues of personal accountability with goodwill as they occur." This intention serves as a guide and a reminder in difficult or intense situations.

You could also choose to work on a relevant technique at the same time, such as those we outlined in chapter 7. Sticking with our "recognizing others as free and accountable" commitment, "framing choices" could be a complementary technique. To develop this skill, you might want to ponder questions such as these:

- How do I typically react when people come to me with problems?

- What can I do to ensure I have a good understanding of what the issues are before I respond?

- How do I respond to others who present difficult issues about circumstances? About me?

- Am I using language for engagement and disclosure or for manipulation?

- How can I engage others as partners in finding solutions?

- How can I check myself and change course when I get invested in getting my own way?

Keep a journal about what you notice, even if it is nothing more than jotting a note or two at the end of the day. What went differently? How did people react? What emotional responses did you wrestle with? What things have the potential to distract you from living out your intention? If you want to up the ante, confide in a few people (or a lot of people), and ask them to give you feedback about what they see you doing differently. Ask them to acknowledge when you live out your intentions well, and to call out behaviors that don't align with your stated commitments.

This is something you can do right now. *You can go first.*

Carl Jung, psychoanalyst, philosopher, and influential thinker, spoke of the power of the individual to transform the world when he said,

> If things go wrong in the world, this is because something is wrong with the individual, because something is wrong with me. *Therefore, if I am sensible, I shall put myself right first. . . .*
>
> In the last analysis, the essential thing is the life of the individual. In our most private and most subjective lives, we are not only the passive witnesses of our age, its sufferers, but also its makers. *We make our own epoch.* [Emphasis added.]

Making our own epoch is a difficult and constant struggle. As the authors of this book, we both know this well and experience it in our daily lives. On a perfect day in April 2006, we turned our faces in a new direction and committed to take full accountability for each other's success and for the success of our relationship, both personal and professional. Even in the short time we have been married, we have been confronted with (and have raised) plenty of difficult issues at work and at home. Life keeps up its irritating tapping on our shoulders, and we get distracted. Occasionally we return to the reassuring comfort of old, familiar behaviors and traditional conversations. Our intention is always to talk to each other with goodwill, and we sometimes falter. We get selfish. We use manipulative language. We say cynical things or cast ourselves as victims. We find ourselves wanting to win. We disappoint each other, and at times we are reluctant to forgive. We get discouraged and wonder at our audacity at writing this book or encouraging others to do something we can't always pull off ourselves. And with time, thankfully, somehow we summon up the will to remember that this is not who we want to be. We find a way to turn to each other again. We climb out of our trenches, clean ourselves up, and recommit to the vows we made on our wedding day. We get back to an authentic conversation.

Our hope is that as a result of reading this book you too will embrace, practice, and live out what many of our clients have as they work toward personal and organizational transformation. Our hope is that commitment and recommitment will keep authentic conversations alive. These conversations benefit us all. They are good for organizations. And they are good for the soul.

A Practical Guide to
Authentic Conversations

Suggestions for Getting Started

Throughout this book we have focused on the intentions, commitments, and skills necessary to change ordinary workplace (or anyplace) conversations from traditional parent–child conversations to authentic conversations among committed, accountable adults. We have focused on accountability, caretaking, betrayal, cynicism, helplessness, and other conditions that create a need for conversations when people face change or other challenges. We have explored the importance of dealing with your own indirect expressions of vulnerability and confronting that resistance in others.

In the following pages, we offer practical guides for authentic conversations that occur thousands of times a day in every workplace. We created these outlines using the commitments and skills contained in this book as a way to help you hear how authentic conversations might sound.

Like life, conversations do not follow a script. They are fluid. They change from moment to moment, situation to situation. Even so, when trying to engage more authentic conversations in an environment where they are not customary, guidelines and outlines can be useful. They can help you clarify your intentions and remind you of the essential skills you must keep at the forefront so that the conversations serve your intention or purpose.

The outlines contain the commitments as reminders (i.e., always maintain goodwill) and the skills as "steps." Being able to combine the skills and commitments on the fly in everyday conversations requires conscious intention, constant attention, and regular use. This change is not casual, but we believe—and our experience backs this up—that it will be well worth the trouble.

Facing a Difficult Issue

Sooner or later, difficult issues require a conversation, and you must confront a fundamental choice about how you engage. You either choose instrumental conversations using language for manipulation, or you choose conversations for engagement using language for disclosure (see chapter 6). If your intention is to pursue freedom, choice, accountability, and collaboration as the foundation for positive change, conversations for engagement serve best. The examples are general to give you ideas. Add details of your own experience in neutral, descriptive words.

When confronting difficult issues, remember the importance of *extending goodwill* as you:

State the reason for the conversation or meeting:

> "As I see it, we're meeting to talk about circumstances surrounding the XYZ project (or our relationship), which have become difficult."

State your intention to resolve the issue or make it work:

> "My intention for getting us together is to figure out a way we can make this work."

Name the difficult issues clearly and directly, without judgment:

> "As I see it, the difficult issue is that you are disappointed with the way this project is proceeding. I have heard from others that your belief is that I am the cause of the difficulty. What is your take on the issue? Tell me more about how you see things."
>
> **OR**

"I want to raise an issue that has become difficult for me. We have lost contact with each other on this project, and as a result, two important deadlines have been missed."

Own your contribution to the difficult issues:

"My contribution to the difficulty is I neglected to address the strain in our relationship when we missed the first deadline. In addition, I have been blaming you for not coming to me. And I seriously dropped the ball by not including you in our last meeting with Andrea's department because I was angry."

Invite engagement and request the help of the other person:

"I really want your help in working this out. You may feel that I caused this mess and now I am asking for your help because there is no alternative. I can understand if you feel that way. Having said that, I still want to work this out together."

Ask for the other person's viewpoint:

"What is your point of view about what has happened with our relationship and its impact on the project?"

Shift responsibility by asking how the other person wants to proceed:

"It sounds like you do think this is my fault and you are still angry with me. How do you think we should proceed here?"

Things to watch out for in this conversation are a desire to win by manipulating the information, threatening, blaming, caretaking, arguing, and prescribing. Most of these things are an outgrowth of your own resistance to facing the difficult situation. Getting clear about what your resistance might be is a useful first step.

People often ask, "When during this conversation do I get to tell them what *they* did wrong?" It is a great question with a tricky answer. Frankly, we would urge you to resist the temptation. No matter how you phrase it, naming someone else's contribution feels to the other person like a traditional conversation of blame. But if you feel you must, do this only after owning your contribution to the difficult issue. If you choose to do this, using neutral language is essential. Remember it is likely people will hear what you say about them much more loudly (and more painfully) than anything you have said about your contribution. Check your motives. What/whose needs are you trying to satisfy? What are your intentions for explicitly pointing out their contributions? How will pointing out their contributions add to the conversation and help to reach a collaborative understanding?

Seeking an Exception

At times you may see a better way to do something but discover that a person, policy, regulation, or relationship prohibits you from trying a different approach. Typically, you might look for a powerful ally and ask his permission or request that he "give you a break" so you can try your approach. That sort of permission-seeking conversation reinforces the parent–child dynamic. You want the person with power to grant you permission, yet he is still on the hook if things don't go well or if you fail.

An alternative is to seek an exception by making a promise for results. Include specifically stated consequences for you if you don't achieve the promised results. Again, *extending goodwill* colors the conversation as you:

State the reason for the meeting:

> "I want to talk with you about our informal policy of having to get your permission to meet with people more than two levels higher than me in the organization."

Identify the exception requested and the (business) reasons for seeking it:

> "I would like an exception. I need to talk to many people in higher positions, including the VPs, in order to successfully complete the projects I am working on. You are very busy and often out of the office. When I have to gain your permission first, it really slows things down."

Acknowledge and support the other person's reservations about accountability and/or consistency:

"The reservations you have make sense to me. This would make me different from the rest of the department, and you are concerned about staying up to date on the projects. That would concern me too, if I were in your position."

Offer a promise for results (and guarantee consequences) in exchange for the exception:

"If we do this, I promise to inform you about progress on my projects on a weekly basis, either with a meeting or a short written report, whichever you prefer. I will also let you know who I am likely to talk with in the upcoming week. However, those things can change rapidly so I'd like the flexibility to respond in the moment. [Consequences:] If you get a major, unwanted surprise doing things this way, I will go back to adhering to the old policy."

Seek agreement:

"What suggestions do you have?"

OR

"Are you willing to give this a try?"

Summarize the agreement or acknowledge differences and request opportunities for further discussion:

"So my understanding of our agreement is . . ."

OR

"It sounds like we can't agree on this today. Are you willing to consider this further? I will get back to you in two days to discuss it."

You can sabotage this conversation by losing your nerve and asking for permission, seeking sponsorship if it is not authentically offered, whining, or portraying yourself as a victim. Being manipulative and bartering will also get in the way. These are mostly the child in you acting out or responding to the parent you see in the other.

The intention of this conversation is to frame the exception-seeking process as an opportunity for collaboration and putting yourself on the hook for accountability if things go wrong.

Proposing Change

Each of us sees opportunities to make changes that could improve the organization. This conversation does not assume any authority tied to title or position. It is a conversation for anyone, but in most traditional organizations today, a manager or supervisor would be most likely to initiate it. The conversation requires enough business literacy that necessary information is available to the individual proposing a change.

Engaging in conversations that build support for these changes can be challenging. Traditionally, you may have remained silent or turned to manipulative language to get your way by "putting a spin" on the information, being indirect, or not telling the whole story. The following conversation is an alternative. *Extend goodwill* as you manage this conversation.

Describe the change you are proposing:

"I'd like to propose revamping the way we admit patients to this hospital through the emergency room."

Give the business reasons for proposing the change:

"About 80 percent of our admissions to this hospital come through the ER. Patients are stacked up in the ER and are actually receiving treatment there that they should be getting upstairs. Our patient satisfaction scores have been declining for the last three months. Patients are complaining, our staff is complaining, and we've been over budget as well."

Outline the difficult issues:

"I realize that this will be a difficult change. ER employees have been pretty territorial about what happens here. We have discouraged others from making suggestions about the way we do things. This change would require serious collaboration among admitting, labs, radiology, environmental services, and transportation. We don't have a history of working cooperatively, so this will be a challenge. Also, I sometimes get frustrated when things get rough. I will have to watch my temper."

Invite and encourage additional reservations:

"What other difficulties do you folks see?"

Extend understanding and agreement:

"It sounds like we all agree that this will be difficult. You raised issues I hadn't thought of."

Frame the choices you see for proceeding:

"It seems like we have two choices here. We can continue what we are doing and watch our results continue to erode. Or we can be willing to face the difficult issues and enlist the help of others who are also connected to this process."

Ask them to frame choices they see:

"Tell me what choices you see."

State your choice:

"I am choosing to move forward by trying to convene a large group from all the involved departments. I am going to find people interested in understanding how we all need to work together in order to resolve the issues so our patients are given a higher standard of care."

OR

"You've raised some good issues that need to be explored before we make these changes. How do you think we should proceed?"

Ask for their decision or acknowledge differences and request opportunities for further discussion:

"I know a lot of you have reservations about this. What choices are you each going to make in supporting this effort?"

OR

"What is the next step for finding a better way to resolve this problem?"

Potential pitfalls include mandating the change (particularly if you are in a position of authority), selling, caretaking, and bartering. When you want your own way, it is sometimes difficult to honor others' conflicting viewpoints and stay focused on your intention of engaging them as adults with choices to make as well.

If you are in a position of authority and use this conversation to influence others without acknowledging the intention to make the change with or without their support, it is manipulative and inauthentic.

If the change under discussion is mandated, use the following conversation. Remember that *extending goodwill* is critical, and resistance is likely to be an issue.

Introducing a Mandate

When regulators, policy makers, or other powerful individuals make nonnegotiable demands that affect employees, you may be asked to engage others in something you don't necessarily (or totally) embrace. Typical conversations in these situations are cynical or framed as helplessness. They create excuses for a lack of accountability. A more authentic conversation deals with accountability head on; it does not look for excuses or ways to work around the mandate. It engages others in legitimate choices. This conversation is similar to the one in chapter 8, which confronts cynicism:

With goodwill, describe the mandate and the business reasons for it:

> "Because our customer satisfaction scores are slipping drastically and, as a result, revenue is way off, auditors have said that we must change our work processes. Changing the processes is not optional."

Clearly state the potential negative impacts and ask others to do the same:

> "This change is expected to have a short-term negative effect on our results while we define the new processes. Negative effects could be long-term if we don't come up with an effective solution. Our attitudes will also be tested, because this will likely be a difficult change."

Ask for acknowledgement of and elaboration on these negative impacts:

"What concerns do you have about what I have said? What other potential negative impacts can you see?"

Extend understanding and validate the objections:

"You've raised a lot of legitimate objections to doing this. I don't necessarily agree with everything each of you has said, but your objections are real and I take them seriously. We definitely have our work cut out for us."

Frame choices about possible responses to the mandate:

"Each of you has a choice to make regarding this mandate and how you will engage it."

State your choice for proceeding in the face of your own objections:

"While I see many difficulties with this situation, my choice is to give this my best. I am committed to working with you to find the best solution, and I am optimistic about our ability to find the best ways to get this done."

Invite others to make the same choice:

"You all have a choice here. I invite you to give it your best. We can use the help and support of everyone to make this work. However, you must decide for yourself what to do. What questions do you have?"

Things to be aware of and avoid in this conversation include colluding with the cynicism or name-dropping ("The senior VP said we have to do this, so we have to get on board"). Also watch out for caretaking, bartering, casting yourself as a bystander, or claiming that you are "only doing my job." Getting clear about your intentions in the situation is critical before engaging others in conversation. Understanding the struggle others will have comes from struggling with the circumstances yourself. No one really likes being told they *must* do something. Processing the possibilities is part of dealing with a mandated situation. If you can't find a way to legitimately support the mandate, this is not the conversation for you.

Renegotiating an Established Relationship

When a relationship is floundering, it may be necessary to start over. Finding a new way of relating or working together can be touchy or uncomfortable. The relationship was established on one set of agreements (implicit or explicit) and now you are saying, "This isn't working, let's try something else." Here is an outline for an authentic conversation for doing this, which assumes that you are engaging the other with goodwill:

State the purpose for the conversation as you see it:

"Thanks for sitting down with me. I want to talk with you about what I see as the troubled nature of our relationship."

Name the difficult issues in the relationship:

"I have noticed our relationship has become combative. Others have noticed it too. We frequently disagree with each other and argue at meetings. We have also done things that have resulted in a sense of mistrust."

Ask for their view of these issues and your contributions to creating them:

"Tell me how you see this situation and what I have done to contribute to you not trusting me. What contributions have I made to our not trusting each other?"

Extend understanding and own your contributions:

"You are right, I did do the things you mentioned. I have a different perspective about some events you mentioned, but I can see your point of view here. Also, I have been talking to other people about you and this situation instead of sitting down with you."

Frame the choices for proceeding as you see them and ask them to do the same:

"The way I see it, we can continue doing what we have been doing and nothing will change. Or we can begin to consciously change how we deal with each other in the name of improving the relationship. What choices do you think we have?"

State your wish and intention to create a new set of agreements for this relationship and name them:

"As long as we're working this closely together, I'd like us to find a way to get along and create a new relationship based on trust. Telling each other the truth will eliminate much of what has been difficult in the past. I am committing to telling you the truth from now on, and coming directly to you when I see problems instead of talking to others."

Ask for their engagement and commitment:

"Would you consider agreeing to telling me the truth as well?"

Negotiate agreement on future steps or seek further opportunities for discussion:

> "I know that this has been a lot of new information in a short conversation. I want you to think about this and let's get back together tomorrow afternoon and see if we can reach an agreement. How do you feel about that?"

Cynicism, distrust, blame, casting yourself as the victim, and bartering will send this conversation off track. It is useful to check your intentions and motives for confronting the situation, and whether you are invested in a specific outcome. If you have specific motives or are invested in an outcome, be honest about those with yourself and others.

Realize that by having this conversation, you are putting the relationship at risk. Grieving and letting go may be important here. Something will be lost—the old way of relating—even if the conversation is successful in renegotiating the relationship.

Initiating Endings

Despite our best efforts, sometimes things just don't work out well. Initiating endings is one of the most difficult conversations we can have. Typically, such conversations are marked by mutual blame and recrimination. This new conversation calls for a focus on extending goodwill, compassion, and directness.

State your wish to consider ending the project or relationship:

"I have been giving this situation a great deal of thought and I want to consider ending this relationship. It has caused us both a great deal of difficulty, and I am not willing to continue like this."

Give solid (business) reasons for ending *and* for continuing:

"My reasons for wanting to end this relationship are . . . I also see a number of reasons for continuing it, such as . . ."

Ask for their view of proceeding with the conversation and their arguments for and against ending the relationship:

"I am curious about how you see things. How do you want to proceed and what are the reasons you see for ending the relationship and for continuing it?"

Extend understanding about areas of agreement and disagreement:

"It seems we agree on some things, like . . . We also have different perspectives on other issues, such as . . ."

State your decision to end (or continue) in spite of your doubts:

"This is very difficult for me, but after talking this over with you, I continue to feel that ending the relationship is the best decision. I have doubts about proceeding this way, but I feel it is what I want to do."

OR

"In light of what you've said, I'm willing to continue the relationship if we can agree on changes that will make it more productive."

Ask for their decision:

"How do you want to proceed?"

Acknowledge their disagreement if it is relevant:

"We don't see this the same way. You want to continue and I don't."

Ask for their view about how to proceed with the ending:

"What specific things should we pay attention to as we proceed?"

Negotiate an agreement, if possible. If no agreement is possible, state how *you* intend to proceed:

"It is clear that this is a very difficult situation for you. Since you don't want to proceed with this, here is what I intend to do . . ."

This conversation can be particularly difficult because of the dissatisfaction with the relationship or project. Things to avoid include blaming others or casting yourself as a victim, prolonging the decision, and/or hesitating because of doubt. While your decision for initiating the ending led to this conversation, it is important to remain open. New information generated during the conversation could influence your previous decision.

Dealing with Individual Performance

In chapter 10, we showed you a conversation for dealing with individual performance issues as you initiate changes or projects. Raising and confronting performance issues are difficult and require the best of us. The conversation is based on the undeniable reality that each person is accountable for his or her own performance. It proposes that you take responsibility for actively seeking feedback on your performance.

Accountability for individual performance is one of the major bastions of formally sanctioning parent–child relationships at work. As adults who manage complex lives at work and outside of work, there is something unnatural about sitting down with someone to find out the three things you need to improve next year. Knowing that your compensation is tied to this process whether you take it seriously or not compounds the problem. The following is a process for doing "formal" appraisals that embodies individual accountability for performance.

A Radical Performance-Appraisal Approach

Performance management historically has been defined by accountability to a boss and compliance with top-down performance measures. Performance management conversations are the epitome of parent–child conversations and a key ingredient in the glue keeping parent–child cultures intact. In a world that values control and consistency, this approach seems reasonable. However, if the intention is to create a culture of commitment and accountability and to treat each other as adults, a new conversation and system are needed to reflect a different intent.

This conversation shapes a new system for assessing performance. The heart of the change is based on the notion of the individual choosing accountability, or making true commitments, to a community (business unit, etc.) as opposed to complying with accountabilities imposed from the top. Establishing this approach means creating circumstances where employees can become literate about the business, understand what is at stake in the marketplace, and see how their performance contributes to success. The process looks like this:

Preparation: Choosing and Inviting

If you are accountable for your performance as it relates to the larger community, you take responsibility for convening an annual performance review committee meeting rather than having it imposed on you. (These meetings could be more frequent, depending on the needs of the business/community.) Convening the meeting means you must do two things:

1. Invite several people (there is no magic in the number) who have the most pertinent feedback on your performance. This could include peers and customers and may or may not include a supervisor or our boss. This is up to you.

2. Chair your performance review committee meeting.

The meeting has three rounds of conversation. Each round has a specific purpose.

Round One: Expressing Your Doubts

Each of us carries to work doubts about our performance and our ability to contribute all that we wish or all that is required. We can *always* find something to work on. In this part of the meeting, you express thoughtful, authentic doubts about your performance. These doubts are connected to results you must achieve, ways you must benefit your unit (or community), or ways you must engage based on the good of the whole.

Invite specific individuals from your committee to share doubts and concerns about your performance. In this round, committee members don't speak unless they are asked for input. You are responsible for gaining clarity and understanding doubts as they are expressed, not defending against them.

Round Two: Making Promises and Choosing Consequences

You construct three or four promises you intend to make to your unit and/or the organization during the interval between formal reviews. The promises should be based upon what you see as your contribution to the overall success of the organization. They should be framed in terms of results or ways in which you must engage. Preparing for this round is critical and reflects the responsibility you have to the business/community. Sometimes distributing the promises in advance is useful, and round two could be staged on a different day than round one.

After promises have been stated, the committee speaks with the "eyes and voice of the business" to affirm, modify, or push back on the promises. Committee members should respond to the promises based on their knowledge and beliefs about the business and whether the promises address the needs of the organization during the upcoming period. Speaking with the "voice of the business" means committee members must talk about how the promises you are making contribute to the greater good. The conversation continues until joint agreement is reached.

In this round, you also talk about the consequences of not keeping your promises. These consequences are framed for yourself (in terms of restricting freedom, restricting access to resources, diminishing opportunities for future influence, etc.) as well as for the organization (customer impact, eroding financial performance and quality, etc.). Create one or two realistic consequences for nondelivery to give concrete credibility to your promises. These are also negotiated with the committee as described above.

Round Three: Publishing Promises

After you have reached agreement on promises and consequences, they are kept in a place that everyone can access. This place contains the promises and consequences of others in your unit and the larger enterprise. The promises can and should be revisited during the period to determine whether they are still relevant to the business. It is your responsibility to see that they are reviewed and reconvene the committee if the promises need to be changed as a result of business changes.

People sometimes say this process seems harsh or depressing because it focuses on doubts, promises, and consequences. They ask why a round for "things done well" isn't included. We are all for celebrating success, giving or getting credit for a job well done, and congratulatory pats on the back. Doing this is important and useful, but it also puts the focus on the past. This process is designed to create a focus on future needs of the business.

Disconnecting "merit pay" from the performance appraisal process is also highly recommended as a way to eliminate parent–child cultures. It makes more sense to align compensation to an employee's contributions to the business and its customers, and to pay for skill acquisition to help strengthen the business.

This process is a guideline and could be altered in a way that fits with your organization as long as the emphasis is on personal accountability rather than holding others accountable. Our experience tells us this type of evaluation gets at one of the most difficult issues in managing performance—the reality that you are the *only* one responsible for *your* performance. How could it be otherwise? This process also eliminates the performance and accountability problems created by traditional appraisal systems, which perpetuate the myth that one person can hold another person accountable.

Creating Your Own Authentic Conversations

Ultimately the goal is to create authentic conversations in the moment as circumstances arise. Once you are using the commitments and skills regularly, the conversations will soon become second nature. However, in the beginning it can be useful to develop your own "conversation guides" to help you keep on track. Keeping your intentions, commitments, and the necessary skills at the forefront in real time is always challenging. Planning and practice are essential in developing these skills. Be aware of opportunities to design your own conversations. You might even stage a rehearsal or enlist a coworker to play a role while you practice. Questions to ask yourself could include:

- What is the purpose of the conversation?
- What is my intention in the conversation?
- What commitments are relevant?
- What skills will be particularly useful?
- What resistance can I expect in myself and the other person?
- What might the conversation sound like?

Acknowledgments

If we were to acknowledge everyone who has contributed to this book, it would take at least another chapter and quite possibly another book. We are indebted to dozens of authors, friends, colleagues, and thinkers, whose ideas, work, and conversations we relied on heavily in formulating these concepts. Several authors who stimulated our thinking and inspired us to take action are cited in this book, but of course, those snippets represent a tiny fraction of their knowledge and wisdom. Some of these writers and thinkers we know only through their printed words. Others we are blessed to know personally. In all cases, their contributions have been truly invaluable. Thank you all.

Though we couldn't possibly name them all, we also have thousands of clients to thank. They have asked profound questions and challenged the concepts, helping us refine and rethink what we thought we knew. They have allowed us to deliver a message, and even if they didn't always embrace it, they left us with lessons learned. They have been generous with their insights. Many have embarked on the journey toward authentic conversations. We are grateful to them for all these gifts.

Other people we can acknowledge by name and are delighted to do so. Thank you, Derek Millard and David Gilmore for providing a serene respite in spectacular surroundings, which allowed us the space and peace we needed to finish the first draft. Your suggestions for improving that draft were also much appreciated. Feedback provided by early readers Larry Dressler, Kathleen Epperson, Tom Heuerman, and Kendra Armer was immensely useful. We appreciate the time and care each of you took with our work. Mike Foley, we are grateful for your grace and generosity. Jayne Sanford is a valued associate, dear friend, and practitioner of these ideas and conversations. She has been with us all along—thank you, Jayne. We also want to acknowledge people who have moved us in such profound ways that these pages are infused with their wisdom, spirit, and practice. Among them are Pat Banks, Jim Burke, Nancy Calle, Will Clayton, Joe Curran, Bob Hall, Kevin Herring, the late Max Jennings, Marge McCollum, Christine Miller, Kathy Neilson, John Nickens, Steve Schreiner, and Sheri Streasick. The folks who have been associated with Designed Learning over the years played a role in the early development of these ideas and concepts, especially the late Jim Maselko, whose faith in them was unwavering.

Judy Henning's friendship, counsel, and love over the years have kept this book alive through some of the most difficult times. Thank you and *namaste*.

Tricia McCarty and Mike Morchak, bless your light-filled hearts. And heartfelt thanks goes to Mary Bruce for her teachings, support, and most especially for the gift of *san culpa*.

We are forever grateful for the love and support of our families, including our parents, James and the late Jean Showkeir, and Maurice and Arlene Bateman. Our children, Sonnet, Skyler, JR, and Zackery, are a constant source of learning and joy, and we rest assured knowing that the future is in their good hands.

Finally, sincere thanks to all the wonderful folks at Berrett-Koehler, especially Steve Piersanti and Jeevan Sivasubramaniam. It has been an honor working with a publisher that built its business on the principles we write about. Your faith in this work and your deft touch with these neophyte authors have been amazing. You have our deep gratitude for making the journey so enjoyable.

Notes

INTRODUCTION, The Dangerous Book for Adults

Schein, Edgar, quoted at http://en.wikipedia.org/wiki/corporate_culture.

Wheatley, Margaret J., *Leadership and the New Science*, 3rd ed. (San Francisco: Berrett-Koehler Publishers, 2006), chap. 7, p. 28.

CHAPTER 1, Revolutionary Conversations for Results

Block, Peter, *The Empowered Manager* (New York: Macmillan/ Jossey-Bass, 1986).

Wagner, Rodd, and Harter, James K., *12: The Elements of Great Managing* (New York: Gallup Press, 2006), pp. ix–xvii.

Ibid., chap. 1, p. 4.

CHAPTER 3, The Myth of Holding Others Accountable

Forward, Gordon, "Chaparral Steel Unleash Workers and Cut Costs," *Fortune*, May 18, 1992.

Laub, Jim, "From Paternalism to the Servant Organization: Expanding the Organizational Leadership Assessment (OLA) Model," *International Journal of Servant Leadership* 1, no. 1 (2005):155–186.

Semler, Ricardo, *Maverick: The Success Story Behind the World's Most Unusual Workplace* (New York: Warner Books, 1995).

Semler, Ricardo, *The Seven-Day Weekend: Changing the Way Work Works* (New York: Portfolio Hardcover, 2004).

Wieners, Brad, "Ricardo Semler: Set Them Free," *CIO Insight*, January 4, 2004.

Taylor, Frederick Winslow, *The Principles of Scientific Management* (New York: Harper and Brothers, 1911), p. 7. Online at http://melbecon.unimelb.edu.au/het/taylor/sciman.htm.

CHAPTER 5, Hostages to Disappointment

Block, Peter, *The Answer to How Is Yes* (San Francisco: Berrett-Koehler Publishers, 2002), chap. 3, p. 43.

CHAPTER 8, Stop Courting the Cynic

Frankl, Viktor, *Man's Search for Meaning*, 3rd ed. (New York: Washington Square Press, 1984), p. 86.

CHAPTER 9, Cutting the Ties That Bind

Argyris, Chris, and Donald Schon, *Theory in Practice: Increasing Professional Effectiveness* (New York: Macmillan/Jossey-Bass, 1974), p. 30.

CHAPTER 11, Open Season—Remove the Camouflage!

Block, Peter, *Flawless Consulting*, 2nd ed. (San Francisco: Pfeiffer, 2000), chap. 8, p. 139.

CONCLUSION, Starting the Revolution

Zohar, Danah, and Ian Marshall, *Spiritual Capital: Wealth We Can Live By* (San Francisco: Berrett-Koehler Publishers, 2004), p. 145.

Further suggested reading that is not cited here can be found at www.henning-showkeir.com.

Index

About the Authors

Jamie Showkeir

Learning has been at the heart of Jamie's life and career from the beginning. His early professions were public school teacher, administrator, and football coach. Since the early 1980s, he has used his expertise to help individuals and organizations improve results while creating workplaces where people find meaning and purpose. His work is grounded in the belief that individual choice must be authentically engaged for organizations to successfully create cultures of accountability.

As a scholarship athlete, Jamie graduated in 1975 from Miami University with a degree in industrial and business education. He earned his master's in educational leadership at Eastern Michigan University. He also got an honorary degree from the School of Harsh Realities when he was pink-slipped as a schoolteacher in Flint, Michigan, after General Motors laid off nearly one-third of the city's population. From that adversity came opportunity: a position that allowed him to create collaborative labor–management relationships as program director of the Buick/United Auto Workers Employee Development Center. After the successful completion of that assignment, Jamie spent several years working in line and staff positions for EDS, TRW, and Ford Motor Company. He began his first consulting business in 1989 and has worked with hundreds of clients—large and small corporations, educational enterprises, nonprofits, and government entities— to strengthen their organizations. During his career, Jamie has trained hundreds of internal and external consultants, helping them become more successful with their clients by focusing on business results.

In the late 1990s, Jamie served as dean and faculty member of the School for Managing and Leading Change. The school provided in-depth, long-term learning primarily based on distributing organizational power for managing successful businesses.

In 2000, Jamie and his partner, the late Joel Henning, combined their extensive educational, business, and consulting experience to create *henning-showkeir & associates, inc.*, using workshops and other resources based on the same premises.

Jamie has a long-standing membership and professional relationship with the Robert Greenleaf Center for Servant Leadership, where he has designed and developed training as well as provided consulting services. Jamie served as president of the Autism Society of Michigan from 1989 to 1992. Serving on numerous nonprofit boards and devoting considerable consulting time and energy to nonprofit organizations, he advocates for people with disabilities to help them find their own voice and place as full members of mainstream society.

Jamie and his wife, Maren, live in Phoenix, Arizona. Together they have four grown children and a grandson. They enjoy yoga, cycling, music, and traveling.

Maren Showkeir

I have long had an affinity for the power of words and cannot remember a time when I didn't love to write. When I was in high school, my mother, an English teacher, offhandedly suggested that I work for the school newspaper. Upon seeing my first byline in Westwood High School's *War Chant*, I was hooked. After graduating from Arizona State University in 1979 with a BA in journalism, I worked in newspapers as a reporter and editor for nearly twenty-five years. Though I managed my career somewhat haphazardly and the work had its attending successes and frustrations, journalism expanded my world in profound ways.

Starting in 2003, I twice had the privilege of serving as a Knight Fellow for the International Center for Journalists (www .icfj.org), whose mission is to promote "quality journalism worldwide in the belief that independent, vigorous media are crucial in improving the human condition." As a fellow, I taught senior-level journalism classes at private universities in Buenos Aires, Argentina, and Lima, Peru. The most rewarding work I did as a fellow was collaborating with local journalists to develop workshops for those in the provinces who had few opportunities for formal training. When I returned to the United States in the summer of 2005, I began looking for work that would continue to feed my soul and make a difference in the world. I barely dared to hope that I would find it.

During my search, a career coach suggested that I interview people in professions where the writing and teaching skills I had acquired would be transferable and could be employed in an environment that aligned with my goals. One of the people I interviewed was Jamie Showkeir.

During that first conversation, Jamie casually mentioned that he'd been struggling to write a book he had started with his partner, Joel Henning, who died unexpectedly in 2001. Would I be at all interested in looking through his materials and seeing if I thought there was a book there?

I was interested.

Those materials articulated ideas I had long believed about the way people should be treated at work and in life. There was a book there. I joined *henning-showkeir & associates, inc.*, as a partner in October 2005, a decision that, once again, expanded my world. In April 2006, Jamie and I married. Between us we have four grown children and a grandson. We are settled in Phoenix, Arizona, only a few miles from the high school where I first aspired to write for a living.

Among the many wonderful things our professional and personal partnership has produced is this book on authentic conversations. My wish is that you will find it useful. Like Margaret J. Wheatley, whose gracious foreword begins this book, I believe that "we can change the world if we just begin listening to each other again."

henning-showkeir & associates, inc.

*Creating organizations that harmonize
the demand for business results with
the individual's need to find
meaning and purpose at work.*

henning-showkeir & associates, inc., was founded by Joel Henning and Jamie Showkeir in 2000 to fulfill this promise. In 2005, Maren joined as a managing partner. Our consulting, training, speaking, and writing are designed to build the capacity of our clients to accomplish that mission. We work solely from the perspective of distributing organizational power and creating partnership as a strategy for managing an enterprise. Our belief is that refining traditional systems that have compliance and command-and-control as their foundation does not work. Such systems have outlived their usefulness and are degrading to the human spirit.

Our consulting strategy is to deliver our expertise in change management, leadership development, and organizational development through collaboration and creating partnerships with you. At *henning-showkeir & associates, inc.*, we are committed to:

- Building your capacity to succeed in today's complex, demanding marketplace.

- Collaborating with you in every phase of our work: design, development, implementation, and outcomes.

- Offering you innovative, powerful methods that increase competence and accountability and are directly tied to improving your business results.

- Telling you the truth when our expertise is not relevant and helping you find the resources you need.

- Raising the difficult issues with goodwill.

Our commitment to results is always backed with a guarantee. If we don't deliver the agreed-upon business results, or you don't find value in our work, you don't pay our fees.
It's that simple.
Our workshops will challenge you in ways that cause you to examine your thinking, confront your reality, and acquire powerful skills for personal transformation and organizational change. This work is not for the faint of heart.

- The Conversations Workshop—
  Moving from Manipulation to Truth and Commitment

- Reinventing Staff Groups—
  Creating a Business within a Business

- Advanced Consulting Skills—
  Delivering Your Expertise and Building Capacity in Your Clients

- Creating Cultures of Accountability—
  Putting Minds, Hearts, and Hands to Work

- Purpose and Profit—
  Building Partnership Capacity

- Business Unit Development—
  Six-Stage Organization Change Process

- Designing Holistic Deliberations—
  Getting the System in the Room

- Leadership for Engagement—
  Creating Partnership in a Bureaucratic Environment

- Servant Leadership—
  Distributing Organizational Power for Results

henning-showkeir & associates, inc.

3117 e. vermont ave.
phoenix, az 85016
602.368.6172 office
602.368.6941 fax
602.717.3105 mobile
www.henning-showkeir.com
info@henning-showkeir.com

About Berrett-Koehler Publishers

Berrett-Koehler is an independent publisher dedicated to an ambitious mission: Creating a World That Works for All.

We believe that to truly create a better world, action is needed at all levels—individual, organizational, and societal. At the individual level, our publications help people align their lives with their values and with their aspirations for a better world. At the organizational level, our publications promote progressive leadership and management practices, socially responsible approaches to business, and humane and effective organizations. At the societal level, our publications advance social and economic justice, shared prosperity, sustainability, and new solutions to national and global issues.

A major theme of our publications is "Opening Up New Space." They challenge conventional thinking, introduce new ideas, and foster positive change. Their common quest is changing the underlying beliefs, mindsets, institutions, and structures that keep generating the same cycles of problems, no matter who our leaders are or what improvement programs we adopt.

We strive to practice what we preach—to operate our publishing company in line with the ideas in our books. At the core of our approach is *stewardship*, which we define as a deep sense of responsibility to administer the company for the benefit of all of our "stakeholder" groups: authors, customers, employees, investors, service providers, and the communities and environment around us.

We are grateful to the thousands of readers, authors, and other friends of the company who consider themselves to be part of the "BK Community." We hope that you, too, will join us in our mission.

Be Connected

Visit Our Website

Go to www.bkconnection.com to read exclusive previews and excerpts of new books, find detailed information on all Berrett-Koehler titles and authors, browse subject-area libraries of books, and get special discounts.

Subscribe to Our Free E-Newsletter

Be the first to hear about new publications, special discount offers, exclusive articles, news about bestsellers, and more! Get on the list for our free e-newsletter by going to www.bkconnection.com.

Get Quantity Discounts

Berrett-Koehler books are available at quantity discounts for orders of ten or more copies. Please call us toll-free at (800) 929-2929 or email us at bkp.orders@aidcvt.com.

Host a Reading Group

For tips on how to form and carry on a book reading group in your workplace or community, see our website at www.bkconnection.com.

Join the BK Community

Thousands of readers of our books have become part of the "BK Community" by participating in events featuring our authors, reviewing draft manuscripts of forthcoming books, spreading the word about their favorite books, and supporting our publishing program in other ways. If you would like to join the BK Community, please contact us at bkcommunity@bkpub.com.